CU00750147

I PLAYED THE WHITE GUY

By Michael Cole

Published in the USA by:
BearManor Media
P O Box 71426
Albany, Georgia 31708
www.bearmanormedia.com

ISBN: 978-1-62933-297-0
BearManor Media, Albany, Georgia
Printed in the United States of America
Book design by Robbie Adkins, www.adkinsconsult.com
Front cover photo by Adrian Carr
Back cover photo: "Our very first P. R. shoot."

Contents

Prologue. vii

Chapter 1 – The Neighborhood 1

Chapter 2 - Sharon 23

Chapter 3 – Summer of Love 28

Chapter 4 - Estelle 37

Chapter 5 – *The Mod Squad* 45

Chapter 6 – You Need a Break 56

Chapter 7 – Fame 60

Photo Gallery. 70

Chapter 8 – Fun & Games 90

Chapter 9 – Paula 94

Chapter 10 - Australia 99

Chapter 11 – Giving Back 102

Chapter 12 – After the Squad. 108

Chapter 13 – Acting Out 110

Chapter 14 – Shelley. 115

Chapter 15 – Betty Ford. 124

Chapter 16 – Sober 133

Epilogue. 137

Episodes and Fan Favorites 141

Acknowledgements 161

DEDICATION

I love you, Shelley.
Without you, none of this would matter.

Ted,
I sought my soul, but my soul I could not see. I sought my God,
but my God eluded me. I sought my brother, and I found all three.
(Anon.)

KALEIDOSCOPE

Life as a kaleidoscope of me . . .

I have wondered about that many times as it became a roar of beautiful colors. At the same time, becoming more confusing. I wanted to break my life open and find out where each piece fit. Which color was I? All of them, at one time or another. Each color a different feeling, emotion. Together, turning in a beautiful, lonely mess.

I was locked inside, scratching and clawing, trying to get out through some creative loophole. That's when I realized, I know why the caged bird sings.

I am the only one who didn't hear the lone tree crash in the forest.

Prologue

"Michael, it's for you. A call from Dallas," one of the crew guys told me during a break in filming.

"Dallas?" I asked. Who the hell could that be?

The newest issue of *TV Guide* magazine had just come out and the three of us—Clarence, Peggy, and I—were on the cover. This was a time when almost everyone who owned a TV bought the guide each week to find out what to watch. So with *The Mod Squad* as the feature story, we were getting a lot of attention.

We were filming that particular morning in the studio, and would later go on location at the beach, near Malibu. That location was the perfect metaphor for this new type of "cop show" that had taken the country by storm. We were unorthodox, we were carefree, and we were unpredictable. *The Mod Squad* became a monster hit when it debuted on ABC in 1968 and I was hanging on tight for the ride of my life. The three of us were described as "one black, one white, and one blonde" and that edgy tag line only helped to fuel the hype and hysteria. Our characters were hip and relatable at a time when young people, counterculture, and rebellion were gaining momentum against the backdrop of an unsupported war and an increasingly unpopular administration.

Thanks to some genius casting by Aaron Spelling and Danny Thomas, our show mirrored those youthful demographics: Peggy Lipton played Julie Barnes, the beautiful and slightly wounded runaway whose mother was a prostitute; Broadway star Clarence Williams III was Lincoln (Linc) Hayes, raised in a tough neighborhood, who had been arrested in the Watts riots. I played Pete Cochran, a rich kid who had been kicked out of his parents' home after being caught stealing and racing a car.

We were a trio of attractive, troubled kids who were now helping the police solve crimes by going places where the cops could never go. We were supervised by Captain Greer, played by Tige Andrews, a gruff but caring father figure for three outcasts who were without a traditional family structure. It was us and our captain against everyone else, and our audience could relate to that, especially during those turbulent times.

The Mod Squad was dealing with social issues never tackled before on prime-time television—race relations, abortion, neglected war vets, drugs, domestic violence—and almost nothing was off the table. As an actor, I found these emotionally charged topics exciting and challenging. Quite a change, since initially I had resisted taking the part when Spelling offered it, telling him, "It sounds stupid and I hope it never gets on the air." I didn't want to play some guy who ratted on other troubled kids.

It didn't matter that I was a struggling actor with no job and no money. I was in my James Dean, *Rebel Without a Cause*, anti-everything phase. Life was tough thus far, growing up dirt poor in Madison, Wisconsin, drinking at a young age, getting into fights, a teenage marriage and fatherhood followed by divorce, and getting in more trouble than any one person should. I had nothing to lose, because I'd never had a lot to begin with. I started out at the bottom and things hadn't changed much. So when I was offered this life-changing role, I almost blew it, but it was my attitude that made Aaron more determined to cast me. Maybe my luck really was changing and my life would be more than a blur of fighting and drinking and bad decisions.

I made my way to the phone. "Hello?"

"Mickey, it's your father," said the smooth, masculine voice on the other end of the line.

I felt the blood run out of my face and my mind started racing. I had an instant flashback to the desperate and disastrous journey my mother, brother, and I had made to Texas when I was about two years old on a futile search for my biological father, the man who had deserted us when I was born.

"My father is dead."

"No . . . this is your real father. I'm calling from Dallas. I wanted to—"

My voice turned to steel. "If I ever see you, or hear from you again, I will fucking kill you. Stay away from me. Stay away from Ma. Stay away from Ted. If you don't, I will kill you."

"Mickey, just let me—"

"Don't ever call me again, you son of a bitch." I put the phone down slowly. I didn't know if what I heard was real. I was in disbelief, shaking on the outside, *raging* inside. That call filled me with loathing and disgust. There was so much history, so much that his abandonment had done to our family.

No one in the cast or crew came near me. They knew better. In my rage, all I wanted to do was what I did best: I wanted to drink. Somehow I kept it together until after we finished shooting, and then, that's exactly what I did.

It was a good thing the bastard hadn't shown up in person. I swear to God, I would've shot him.

Chapter 1 – The Neighborhood

I've had and didn't have everything in life from the day I was born, July 3, 1940, in Madison, Wisconsin. One thing was missing from the beginning—I never knew my biological father because the son of a bitch abandoned us when I was born. He left our Ma without a dime, to raise me and my brother, Ted, a year and a half older. That will give you something to think about, and something to feel for the rest of your life. At least, it did me. I've been trying to fill that hole ever since.

Madison is unique, because it is surrounded by two lakes, Lake Mendota and Lake Monona. This historic Native American area includes a small strip of land called an isthmus that runs between the two bodies of water which are joined by the Yahara River, east of downtown. Where I lived, in East Madison, there were plenty of factories and docks. I remember, in particular, the big Oscar Meyer plant that was great for providing jobs, but also for creating an odor from those gigantic smoke stacks that sometimes was enough to gag you. Many of the families in the area emigrated from European countries like Germany, Norway, and Ireland, where my ancestors came from.

My mother, Ted, and I lived with our Grandma Nana during the first three or four years of my life. The neighborhood had more than its fair share of bars, factories, bars, churches . . . and more bars. You could always find a greasy spoon run by a local family trying to make ends meet.

Train tracks ran down the middle of the street by Nana's house. Every once in a while, a train would go slowly by and shake the walls like an earthquake. On another set of tracks about a block away, I could hear the haunting whistle in the middle of the night. I always wondered where the train was going. Like a Johnny Cash song, "I could hear it calling." My earliest memories are wanting to be on that train, wondering where it would take me.

There was a big marsh across the street from Nana's house, and on the hot summer days, Ted and I would often go down to catch frogs and snakes, or we would explore the riverbed and build forts behind the bowling alley. We were inseparable. We needed each other. We were all we had. I can't ever remember our having a single fight.

The winters in Madison were treacherous. It would often drop to twenty degrees or more below zero. We had little heat, which came from a pot-bellied coal stove that Ted and I had to empty and fill each day. There was one tap where we could only draw cold water. We would heat a pot on the stove for washing up and taking a bath—in the sink. There was a toilet in the cellar that froze from time to time, forcing us to just go outside or hike down to the gas station on the corner.

Ted and I shared a tiny bedroom in the attic, with the occasional bat flitting about just as we were trying to go to sleep. We would pull the covers up over our heads, scared shitless. There was also a storage room up there that was ominous. I was convinced monsters lived there.

Ma worked hard at any job she could find, wanting her boys to be clean and nicely dressed. We were deeply loved. She even took some jobs that meant she worked the night shift. I remember I would wait and watch out the bedroom window for her to come home. Sometimes I would wait there till daylight. I was always worried that something might happen to her. I wasn't sure what, but I just knew we couldn't exist without her. The three of us survived because of our love, and our intense need for one another. That's what got us through the hardest times, like when we had to sell Ted's bed for a dime.

When Ma worked nights, and Nana was in charge, I could sometimes be a bit sassy to her. She'd grab her broom and try to catch me so she could whack me with it. I knew she couldn't get up the stairs so I would dash up there, two at a time, until I reached the landing of the attic. She'd be yelling, "You little pup! Wait till your mother gets home!" Of course I knew by then Nana would be fast asleep.

I think maybe I was a little afraid of Nana because of a story she told us. She had chickens in the backyard. One day she spotted a weasel near the hen house. She grabbed a hatchet and stood about ten yards away, and BAM! She threw that hatchet and nailed that weasel. All the chickens were safe. Those eggs were important!

Nana was quite a woman. She raised a total of six kids, Ma being the youngest. Nana's husband, Grandpa Hyland, was a painter by trade. He came from Dublin and his brogue was very strong. He passed away before Ted and I were born, but we heard stories about how every day after work, he would come staggering down the train tracks, singing Irish tunes at the top of his lungs. Drunker than hell.

When I was still a toddler, about three years old, Ma came home one day with some news. She announced she had train tickets. We were going to Dallas (what's Dallas?) in search of our father. Since he deserted us before I was even born, all I knew about him was that he didn't give a shit about us. Sometimes before I'd fall asleep, I'd ask Ted what he was like, but I'd never get much of a response. I don't know if he didn't remember, or didn't want to care, so I tried not to ask too many questions. But it ate at me inside. Why did he leave us? Why did he not want me? Fathers love their kids. Was it my fault? I didn't understand.

My "father" was in the military and stationed somewhere near Dallas. Apparently Ma had either heard from him or been told that he was there. I'm not sure about the details, but I knew she was determined to find him.

Being on a train was an adventure! It was exciting, especially after hearing them rattle by our house every day. I loved being on the inside, watching the countryside zoom by outside. It provided me endless entertainment and my imagination ran wild. I was fascinated by the houses, I guess because we never had one. I loved seeing the towns, and yards with kids running and playing, each one a complete family. Maybe pretty soon I would have one too.

Once we arrived in Dallas, our hopes quickly dwindled. Ma followed up on every lead to no avail. We were staying in a small, rundown motel room, and our money quickly ran out, leaving us stranded and far from home. Even though I was only three, I could sense Ma's disappointment and hurt. I'd never seen her like that.

Not one to be defeated, though, Ma got a job selling peanuts at the Cotton Bowl. She was a tall, striking woman with features of her Irish heritage, so I'm guessing the vendors figured men would eagerly buy a snack from a pretty lady. It must have taken her so much courage to keep going with two small, frightened boys clinging to her. Eventually we had the money for the trip back home.

We were on the train again, but this time the mood was much more somber. Our mission had not been successful and we weren't sure what was next for us except going back to Madison. I was still not sure why my father was so difficult to locate. I wanted so much to make Ma happy, so I thought maybe I could find him on the train, and I decided I should look. I was able to slip away while Ma was dozing, and somehow, I got one of the doors between the train cars open. Then the door slammed shut behind me and I found myself trapped on the small metal platform that connected the two train cars. Both doors were closed, and I had nowhere to go. The wind was whipping around me and I leaned tight against the cold metal door, holding on as tight as I could, hoping somehow it would open. Then I heard a familiar voice on the other side.

"Where's Mickey? Help me find my son!" My mother was screaming and I tried to pound on the door so she would hear me. Suddenly the door slid open and I tumbled inside. "Oh my God, Mickey, are you all right?" I was swooped up into my mother's arms and surrounded by the other passengers who had joined the search. I'll always think of this as my first stunt . . . or my first attempt at running away.

As we made our way back to our seats, the other folks on the train settled down and I looked up at Ma. She was so relieved to have me safe with her that maybe it took her mind off the fact that we were on our way back, alone. The dream had died.

Shortly after our return to Madison, I got very sick. I had a pain in my side, I was vomiting, and I had a high fever. We were lucky that Nana lived next door to a doctor, Dr. Morale. Ma raced me over to see him. He felt my stomach, took one look at Ma and said, "Get Mickey to the hospital at the University of Wisconsin now! He may have a ruptured appendix and peritonitis could be throughout his system."

She rushed me to the hospital with no time to waste. I was whisked into the emergency room and then to surgery. In those day, they gave you ether to knock you out and I can still remember that smell and the mask they put over my nose and mouth. Fortunately they were able to remove my appendix and ensure that the infection had not spread.

Ted and I were so bonded, and he was so worried about me, that he developed what they called a "sympathetic attack." As a precaution, he too was admitted to the hospital. Once they determined that he didn't have appendicitis, they decided to keep him anyway, and set him up in a bed they placed crossways at the foot of mine. Right away I started to feel better. We talked and joked, and even played with some toy soldiers together to pass the time. I remember pretending that one of them was a good guy, and our real father, only the toy was just that . . . a toy. Anyway, in a few days we both felt better. Ma came to get us and the three of us went back to Nana's.

As I got older, the hole left in my heart never healed, but instead seemed to grow bigger and bigger with each passing year. I suppose I was aching for the thing I didn't have. I saw the other kids in the neighborhood with their dads. Sure, they'd complain about their old man and what a hard-ass he was, but for some reason that only made me ache for the same relationship. I just felt that if my father had stayed around, if he had been in our lives, things would have been very different. I was sure of it. He would have provided for his family, or at least taken some of the burden off Ma. But he didn't. He abandoned us; he didn't give a shit about us. I went from hurt to simmering anger to a chip on my shoulder for years to come.

I had plenty of time to think about all this and eventually I came up with a way to make myself feel a bit better. I created my own imaginary family. Maybe I went a bit overboard, but not only did I have the smartest, most awesome father, I also had twenty-eight brothers and sisters, two sets of grandparents, and countless aunts, uncles and cousins. They all had names and personalities and occupations. I put a lot of thought into my new family because I figured if I could create whatever I wanted, it was gonna be great!

When I think back to that time, two things come to mind. First, it might have been the start of realizing that loneliness was my one true companion. It was the one constant that would be loyal and never leave me as my father had. Second, it was probably the beginning of my immersion into make-believe. It's when I realized that just by using my imagination—by summoning up feelings and creating new experiences in my mind, I was able to transport myself. No longer was I stuck in Nana's small, scary attic listening to the jarring sounds of horns honking and neighbors arguing. Now I was surrounded by many family members, all willing to stick by me and help me feel better when I was down. My imaginary family had some definite characters too, just like any family. I wanted them to be realistic after all, and I loved them all just the same. They helped me escape lonely times and in some way, even built my confidence. While this was little more than the active imagination of a lonely, frightened boy, somehow it helped me escape from the tough reality of my circumstances.

After many small jobs, Ma finally got work at a clothing store. My brother and I would occasionally model some of the clothes for the store and get our pictures taken in front of the capitol building in Madison. They'd put us in little camel overcoats and hats, and sometimes Ma would get to keep some of the clothes as payment. That was a big help since we didn't have the money to buy anything new. But during times like that, when we would think things were actually improving, reality would smack us upside the head with a two-by-four.

Like many towns back then just after the Depression, there always seemed to be some rich guy who owned the lion's share of everything. And that guy was usually an asshole. We had one of our very own, a man who owned most of the houses in the neighborhood and the bank, a block away. He seemed to wreak havoc on the lives of everyone I knew because we were all poor. When someone fell on hard times, it was almost impossible to recover. When you couldn't pay your rent, he evicted you. That was it. And that's what happened to Nana. Ma was working hard to try to keep our heads above water, but it wasn't enough. In no time flat, we were out on our asses. I couldn't believe that someone could be that mean, or that things could get any worse for us, but they sure as hell did. Without that home base, our place to gather, we were forced to split up amongst relatives. Ted and I were shuffled from one set of kin to the next, wearing out our welcome along the way. It's not that we were trouble or anything, it was just that everyone was already bursting at the seams so they could only handle the extra mouths to feed for so long. We would stay for a little while, but then we would be off to the next home. It was a very unhappy time. I never felt safe or carefree. I was filled with fear and confusion. Soon Nana went to an old folks' home. She had no choice.

I did my best to adjust to all this, but I was a just a boy forced with trying to cope with grown-up feelings. All I could think of was being back with Ma and Ted again. We didn't stop trying. It seemed like forever, but the three of us finally got back together again. This was the happiest I had felt in a long time. I was so relieved that once again we were living under the same roof in a small apartment.

The next few years were ok. I guess it was kind of a Huck Finn time. It's not easy to get into trouble in a small community like the East side, since everyone knows who you are, but my gang of pals and I sure gave it a try. We would pass the time challenging or daring each other to do something crazy.

In the winter, we sometimes had to shovel our way out of the house because the snow was so deep. But that meant there were great toboggan hills as well. One time we were sliding like hell down a hill and I didn't know there was a barbed wire fence under the snow drift. Whack! The guy in the front got his nose practically sliced off. Luckily it was so cold he just put it in place and it froze back on till he got to the doctor. We built snow forts and threw snowballs at the city buses. Points if you hit the window! Later, when the snow began to melt, we staked out parking meters to search for coins that might have dropped in the snow due to the gloves or mittens everyone wore.

Once the weather warmed up, we swam in the lakes and went fishing with bamboo poles. Many times we needed to catch a fish so we could have supper that night. The first fish I ever caught was a blue gill, the size of a sardine. Ma, with her great sense of humor, made me clean it and then she said she would fry it so I could eat it. By the time I finished cleaning it, though, there wasn't much left. But we both played along. I ate it in one bite and Ma asked me if I was full. "Stuffed, Ma." We laughed like hell.

During the summer heat, an ice truck would come by, because back then people like us still had ice boxes, not refrigerators. As a treat, the driver would stop and chip off a big piece of ice and give it to us. When the weather got really hot, we'd put a chunk of that ice in our pants. Man, did that help! Even if it looked like we wet our pants, we didn't care.

Another one of our favorite things to do was, if we found a penny, put it on the railroad track and watch it get flattened when the train went by. It was a rush, holding the warm metal after the train ran over it. Plus, it was twice as big. Maybe it would be worth twice as much?

When I was around eight or nine years old, I managed to find some unlocked tractors behind the old International Harvester building by the river. Of course I didn't have a clue how to drive one, but why would that stop me? I snuck over to where those tractors were and climbed up on one of them. The key was dangling from the ignition, so I gave it a turn to see what would happen. The old tractor sputtered to life and sat there, chugging and gasping, until I managed to nudge it in gear. Sure as hell I went right into the river because I couldn't stop the damn thing. I couldn't reach the pedals and see where I was going at the same time. I didn't stand a chance. I had to bail from the sinking hunk of metal and swim back to shore. I stood and watched it sink to the bottom. How the police didn't get me for that I'll never know. In a farming state like Wisconsin, stealing someone's tractor is worse than taking a Rolls-Royce!

Next to the marsh there was a warehouse with a cyclone fence that did its best to keep us kids out. But we weren't going to miss the chance to take the empty soda bottles stacked up there. We would simply burrow under the fence and collect as many as we could carry. You got three cents a bottle, and for kids like us, that was a hell of a lot of cash.

My buddies and I passed the time as best we could, sometimes by building cars out of orange crates and baby buggies and then taking turns careening down the hills of an empty street. My first crash happened as I tried to control one of our contraptions while it hurled down the road until I finally crashed! I ended up with lots of cuts and bruises. Just like me, those makeshift cars never had any brakes.

* * *

Ma was big on church and we attended regularly. She was devout, and taught us the church was about love. But every time we'd go, I felt the opposite was true. It wasn't loving—it was scary. I'd already had one father that had left us on our ass, and these priests— "fathers"—frightened me. I never got any comfort from church. So, just as I had done with my imaginary family, I created a truly caring, understanding presence in my life that to this day, I refer to as "my buddy Christ." He continues to provide me support and guidance. But even He couldn't help with the trouble our family experienced within the church.

I think I was about nine years old when Ma received news from the Irish Catholic Church that she, who to me and Ted was approaching Sainthood, was to be *excommunicated!* She had made the choice to divorce the husband who had abandoned her, and that was something the church would not condone. Everyone knew our situation so there was no hiding it. Back then divorce was practically unheard of, and even at my very young age, I felt that we were judged and ostracized. *Those poor boys with no father and the tall, pretty lady who couldn't find her own husband.*

In spite of it all, Ma continued to make Ted and me go to church, even though she couldn't go with us. I felt like everyone stared at us when we walked in. We had so little money we could rarely contribute to the collection plate when it was passed. Sometimes I'd pretend to put something in, but I wasn't fooling anyone. If I did have a penny or a nickel to drop in, it made such a loud pinging sound that I'd instantly regret it. I knew everyone could hear that small contribution echo through the church!

I suppose the teachings of the church had some effect because once I stole a ten-dollar roll of dimes from someone's house. That was a lot of money and I thought of all the things I could buy with it. But it ate at me, and I kept thinking how it would hurt Ma if she found out. I ended up giving it back, knowing the owners would need it to buy food, and confessing this in church. It was one time that I didn't have to make up a sin.

When the church told Ma she was no longer welcome, we were very frightened! And this is exactly what the Church wanted to do! When you hear priests talk about "eternal damnation," who wouldn't be scared? I had all kinds of crazy thoughts. Did you ever burn yourself from fucking around with matches? Well, *this burning would be **forever**. This is what God would do to you if you sinned and didn't confess it. Even the Holy Water to bless you wouldn't work anymore.*

So Ted and I went to mass on Sundays and of course every Christmas Eve. We were "allowed" to be baptized even though we had a divorced mother. What kind of bullshit is that? They also allowed us to take Holy Communion. I was always afraid the little round wafer would get stuck on the roof of my mouth. Sure as hell, many times I had to scrape the "body of Christ" off with a dirty fingernail before swallowing it with a gulp. Ted and I tried to keep up our spiritual duties because we knew how important it was to Ma, but I just couldn't get past the hypocrisy of preaching love and acceptance while shunning Ma, someone who was truly devoted. It made no sense to me. It wasn't fair.

During the Christmas Eve service, there would always be people who passed out. I could tell they were drunk from the smell of alcohol. The "show" was in Latin, which, of course, nobody understood. It was only after mass, walking home, that I truly sensed God. It was because of nature. I enjoyed the magic of fresh snowfall. There was a sense of awe—where did it come from? I loved to hear the crunch of our footsteps, the sound of the church bells, and the smell of the pines. The lights from the bars and streetlights reflected on the snow and it would remind me of the beautiful stained glass inside the church. These were the real moments I felt the Holy Spirit. Things seemed as they should be, peaceful on the eve of Christ's birthday.

Ma would be so happy when we'd get home and describe everything to her. I would go into great detail, holding her attention as long as I could, watching the happiness consume and warm her spirit. She really took comfort from that. But for me, those feelings were fleeting because I couldn't forget what the church had done to her. How could the church do something so horrible? Things were backward. Many of the priests should have been going to confession to ask *her* for forgiveness.

As for Christmas, when I think back, I feel a sense of mystery tinged with a little sadness mixed in. Even the lights and the beautiful music were missing something. I'm not saying Christmas was sad, because we had each other, but it always reminded me we weren't a complete family.

We were able to get a Christmas tree because there was a tree lot right by the marsh across the tracks from Nana's house. Ted and I would help the guy who owned it unload the trees and he in turn gave us one a few days before Christmas Eve. That was exciting! We had a few lights and some tinsel, which my brother would string one strand at a time. Ted would be very careful because of the coal stove we had to keep going for heat. At school we made ornaments and always a star for the top. Like any kid, I guess, I had a question about Santa and coming down the chimney. We didn't have one! Ma wouldn't lie; she would simply smile and say that's how magical Santa really was. That was fine with me. Of course, there weren't many presents, but mine always had something to do with art and pictures of animals that I could draw. One year Ted and I got a game called electric football, which we loved and played for hours on end. We would go to the store where mom worked and some of the ladies that worked with her gave us a set of mittens and a scarf that we could give Ma. We were so proud to have a present for her.

One of my favorite holiday memories is of one of the department stores that had a big Lionel train set up in the window, with little towns, and trees, and houses and people. You would stand in line in the cold and wait for your turn to throw the switch to run the train a few times around the track and make it whistle. I would watch that train and again, dream of the faraway places it could take me.

***

You might think a five-year-old kid would be excited to start school, but not me. I couldn't stand the thought of being "locked in" from morning till night. In fact, I actually skipped my first day of kindergarten. Ted and I had walked to school together, and when we got there, he pointed to where I should go. The school was divided into two sections, one for kindergartners and the other for the rest of the grades. But there were two kindergarten class-rooms, and I accidentally went to the wrong one. They didn't have my name . . . and I really didn't want to be there anyway, so I told myself, *no name . . . no body*!

I went back outside and sat in the middle of the playground wait-ing the entire day until Ted got out and we could go home. Sitting there alone, I heard a plane overhead. Even at that early age, all I could think of was wishing that me and my make-believe family were on that plane, going anywhere except where I was. Of course, Ma made me go back to school the next day. I remember my buddy got thrown out of class because he failed at "nap"! He wouldn't take one! I liked when we created plays and puppet shows, but mostly I hated having to stay in my seat and "behave."

As I got older, it wasn't school that I couldn't stand. It was the authority that some of the teachers exercised over the students. It was more about obeying the rules and how long your hair was than about teaching and inspiring us, about capturing our imagination so we'd want to be there and to learn. What made it worse, I had to go to a new school almost every year because of our moving around so much. That meant many "first days" and never having real friends for long. I hated walking into class that first day, everyone staring at the new kid. It was fucking hard. I never felt I fit in.

As close as Ted and I were, we couldn't have been more different when it came to school. Ted was a natural, gifted student. Learning came easy for him. I could see how proud Ma was of him when he won academic awards, and I was too. At the same time, I was frus-trated because I couldn't live up to his standards. That was not Ted's intention; he would never want me to feel bad. But I did. I would often run away from home in those days, and Ted would find me alone in the dark under a bridge by the river. He'd bring me food. He never criticized me, teased me, or said a negative word; he was just there. I love my brother.

Though I wasn't a good student, and skipped school often, I admired several of my teachers who really cared. I knew they were trying to help me and make a difference, although it hadn't worked. In particular I loved my two art teachers. They would let me come back to the school at night to work on art projects.

We would get rolls of old newsprint from the *Wisconsin State Journal* or I'd use butcher paper and I'd roll the paper down the hallway and paint the backdrops for the school plays. One I remember was of the Paris skyline. It was a tiring piece of work, but I was so proud of it once it was complete. And when I wasn't painting the stage sets, I'd paint and sculpt on my own. Some of my work was featured on local TV, and it was displayed in glass cases at different schools in the area. To top it off, I even sold some. Deep inside my creative juices were stirring.

Then Ma met Lorell, and everything changed.

***

Lorell (pronounced lore-all) was a big guy, probably about six two, and he definitely had a presence about him. He reminded me a bit of John Wayne; he had that type of swagger and confidence. When he and Ma met, he had a good job at Westinghouse as a salesman and he was also in the Army reserve.

Sometimes after work at her job with the clothing store downtown, Ma would join a group of friends and go next door to a hotel bar to socialize. Apparently that's where she met him, and it was obvious they liked each other. When he started coming over more frequently, I could see it was getting serious, at least for him. I always thought in the back of my mind that Ma may have been in love, but I also knew that she wanted to better our living situation, and this was her chance. She wanted us to live in a house and finally feel settled. She wanted to give her boys the security and stability we longed for. We'd never had a place of our very own.

After a year or so, Ma and Lorell were married. They just came home one day and said they had gotten hitched! It took a bit of getting used to because I realized then that Lorell was going to be an important part of Ma's life whether I liked it or not.

We moved into his bachelor apartment in a small building near the University of Wisconsin and lived there for about a year. Then he moved us into a really nice house, and Ma couldn't have been happier. This one was plenty big, and we loved it, although I was reluctant to admit it to Lorell. Ted and I once again shared a room. We had bunk beds that we had sawed in two to make twin beds since we didn't want to argue about who got the top bunk. We were proud that we were able to work out any disagreement that easily.

As time went on I could tell Ma and Lorell were very much in love. It was good to see Ma this happy, but things weren't so good for me. I didn't like sharing Ma, and I didn't like having to answer to Lorell. I had been left to make most of my own decisions up to that point. Now I had to answer to him, and he had a lot of rules. Back then, and maybe for most of my life, rules and I didn't really get along. Now, if I wasn't home by 6:00 I didn't get dinner. If the snow on the driveway wasn't shoveled or the grass in the yard not cut to his liking, I wasn't allowed to leave the house. He was demanding and hard and on me from the start and I resented his control. I guess I should have been grateful when Lorell decided to legally adopt me and Ted, but it meant nothing to me. In fact, I hated the idea. I couldn't grasp the concept that I had my own last name one day and then the next day it wasn't mine anymore.

In hindsight, I realize that Lorell was trying his best. He was a decent man, he worked hard, and provided for his new family. His military-style discipline was probably what I needed, but as a fourteen-year-old boy I resented him, and we clashed often. I felt robbed of Ma's attention, plus I was ordered around. That authority shit pissed me off and I fought it openly. As my relationship with Lorell grew more and more contentious and turbulent, I grew more rebellious and angry. I didn't have to answer to him. He wasn't my father. This was the start of my getting into more serious trouble.

On the other hand, Lorell respected Ted and how hard he worked. Ted excelled at his studies. Lorell was proud of that and often spoke of the great future Ted would have while saying nothing about my admittedly dim prospects. In addition to academics, Ted was in a group called the C Scouts which was "on the water" Boy Scouts. With all the demands of school, and his outside activities, Ted was often away from the house, and didn't have to deal with the new discipline the way I did. Besides, I was confrontational and Ted never was. He internalized his feelings while I spewed out mine.

Whether it was because of all the instability in my early home life, the fact that I hated school, or simply the need to escape, I had been experimenting with alcohol for years. It's no exaggeration to say that I was probably on the road to being an alcoholic by the time I was twelve years old.

I was fifteen when we found out Ma was pregnant, something she and Lorell had both wanted desperately. Ted was away in Europe on a school exchange program, so I had no buffer. It was just me and Ma—and my stepfather. Our relationship had gotten progressively worse; we fought all the time, and I grew more and more defiant. At one point, we got into a vicious argument, yelling and screaming and swearing at each other. It escalated to the point where Lorell went and got a .45 from his nightstand drawer and aimed it at me. Ma was about six months along. She was crying hysterically as I stared at the gun. It was just me and him facing off, but I wasn't afraid. I wasn't scared of him or his gun, I was angry!

I shouted, "Put the gun away, you asshole! She's going to lose the baby! Is that what you want?" He looked over at Ma curled up in the corner of the room sobbing and he eased the gun down on the table. I ran over and held Ma tightly. I could see what our fighting was doing to her.

When he put the gun away, the rules were set: I'd stay away from him and he'd leave me be. I'd come and go through a back window in Ted's and my room to avoid him. I was always happiest when my big brother was at home. At least then I had a friend close by.

One night I came home after getting in a fight with the local Golden Gloves champion (my recommendation is to never do that). I had a black eye, and my nose was bloodied and nearly broken. Of course I was drunk, so I snuck in through the window and fell asleep with a stash of wine bottles under my bed. The next morning, Ted took one look at me and knew what had happened. He got me in the bathroom, cleaned me up, and even washed my pillow case so Ma wouldn't freak out. She didn't need any more drama during her pregnancy. He threw the wine bottles out that "escape window" to keep Lorell from finding them in our room.

Except for the shiner all was ok. Ma more or less understood the eye. After all, I had been in what was called the Badger Boxer program, where boxing coaches from the University of Wisconsin would work with kids in the neighborhood to help them stay out of trouble. She had seen me scuffed up plenty of times. I was proud of the fact that, even though I got some scrapes, I never lost a fight ... well maybe one or two. That was mainly because the gloves were regulation and so heavy that I'd hurry up and try to win so I could take them off! I had a reputation in the neighborhood as a kid that you shouldn't mess with me unless you were ready to see it through.

Lorell was away at army camp, and Ted was away on his exchange program in Europe when Ma was due. I liked it being just me and Ma. I was the man of the house. I was raking or doing something in the yard when I heard Ma scream out in pain. I ran in to the house to find her leaning over a chair, and a pool of blood and water on the bathroom floor. Her water broke and it was time for the baby to arrive!

We had all been waiting for this moment, and I had definitely warmed up to the idea. Maybe this was just what our family needed—what Ma and Lorell needed. I know he was hoping for a boy because he often told us he wanted "one of his own." That didn't help our relationship.

We had to get her to the hospital fast, so I ran over to our neighbor who had a car, and she drove us there. I couldn't bear seeing Ma in pain. When we arrived, the gravity of the situation became clear. Something was very wrong. They rushed Ma into the emergency room. I insisted on staying by her side and praying with her. I summoned the strength of my buddy Christ to get us through this safely. But the doctors couldn't save the baby. She was born with the umbilical cord wrapped around her neck—stillborn. I couldn't believe the beautiful baby girl Ma had always hoped for was gone. We were in a haze of grief. I don't even remember when or how we got home.

I do remember how much we cried when we brought the little empty baby blanket in to what was to have been the baby's room. I tried to comfort Ma. Until that moment, I hadn't known how much emptiness a person could feel inside. Ma and I silently took down the crib. The two of us put away all of the new baby clothes, diapers, toys, and formula—essential supplies that had been arranged in eager anticipation of the arrival. I was trying to be "the man" holding it together, but inside I was just a boy who longed to be comforted too.

This loss only fueled my drinking. I felt guilty that my fights with Lorell had somehow agitated the pregnancy. I felt in some way responsible. Thankfully in a couple of years Ma gave birth to two beautiful baby girls, Deborah and Colleen, about a year and a half apart. They brought joy where there had been sadness. The painful memory of the lost child seemed to dissipate with time, but her death and that empty room stayed with me; haunted me. One more loss to add to the list.

By now, I was sneaking booze from wherever I could find it. I even stole from the liquor store by our house. Often I wouldn't come home. I'd hang out with buddies of mine, other guys from the neighborhood who were restless and bored just like me. One of my good friends was a handsome black guy named Diggs. He was likable and charismatic and he wore one gold earring, which I thought was very cool.

One Saturday night, we were supposed to meet at a bar where we usually hung out, but Diggs asked me to wait for him at a different place. I wasn't sure why, but I figured he had his reasons. I waited for about two hours, but he didn't show up. Diggs was never one to go back on his word. If he said he would be somewhere, then he'd be there. But he was a no-show, and something didn't feel right. I considered going to the bar to look for him, but I remembered he had specifically asked me not to go there. Without him around, I decided to call it a night and head home.

The next morning I found out that Diggs and a couple of older guys newly out of prison had met up at that bar and had decided to rob a sporting goods store, where they stole several guns. The cops were after them and the night ended with a shootout in a local field. Diggs was not hurt, but the other guys were; they all were arrested. Diggs knew there was going to be trouble that night and he made sure that I would be far away from it. I thank him and my buddy Christ for looking out for me.

In the middle of my eighth-grade year of junior high, Lorell announced we would be moving again in a couple of months, but this time, it was away from Madison to Milwaukee. He had gotten a new position with Westinghouse. I knew one thing: I didn't want to go, but I didn't have a choice. I was fifteen years old, and I was drinking a lot. My grades had gone from A's to F's. I had caused a lot of trouble in school, but as the time to leave grew closer, I wanted to say goodbye to a few of my teachers and tell them they were right to have failed me because I didn't do the work. Hell, I wasn't even in class most of the time. Despite of all the trouble I had caused, they wished me well. Most importantly, I needed to thank my two art teachers. I don't know what I would have done without them.

As the move got down to the wire, all I could think about was how I'd miss hanging out downtown with my buddies. State Street comes off the Wisconsin state capitol building in the middle of town, and back then there were about three blocks of the main street that spider-legged off the Capitol Square. That is the area where my friends and I would go, trying to relieve our never-ending boredom. Drinking was our outlet.

You could drink beer in Wisconsin when you were eighteen, but we found plenty of bars that didn't give a shit how old you were. A couple of these places were on State Street. In Wisconsin, it's a big deal to be able to hold your liquor. Beer and Wisconsin are synonymous. Schlitz and Pabst Blue Ribbon. I drank because I wanted and needed an escape. And, at that time, if you were cool and tough, you drank a lot. That earned you respect, and that was a big deal. I also drank because it made me feel invulnerable. I wasn't afraid of a goddamned soul, except maybe my own.

I hated the thought of leaving my closest friends behind. There was Faith. What a great name for her. Everyone loved and respected this beautiful, strong-willed girl. In the eighth or ninth grade, she didn't show up at school one day. (Of course, I never did.) But the news travelled fast that Faith had gotten polio—the horrible disease that was an epidemic in those days. She was confined to an iron lung. But Faith never missed a beat. When she got out of that thing, and into a wheelchair, she went to dances, had boyfriends, drank beer, and kept up in school.

I will never forget one New Year's Eve when a buddy and I went over to spend the night with her. By midnight, more and more pals stopped by. Her mother was great to all of us. We must have listened to Elvis's "Don't be Cruel" 500 times, and probably drank

500 beers. Some of us stayed there till the early morning just to be with this wonderful girl.

Then there was Ralph. He was a smaller guy and, because of it, became the perfect target for school bullies. His last name started with "C," just like mine, so we were in the same homeroom. Almost every day, some asshole would run into him and knock his books all over the floor on purpose, just to be mean and embarrass him. Ralph would fight back tears. I had enough of seeing this shit, and one day I helped him pick up his stuff and I walked him to his next class.

It meant so much to him and he thanked me. "It's cool, Ralph. That son of a bitch is never going to touch you again. I promise." One of my buddies and I found the guy the next day. One punch and the bastard went flying down the stairwell! What was really great was that this bully's girlfriend saw the whole thing. Ralph went on the University of Wisconsin and became a nuclear engineer, scientist, and professor.

All my life I've been for the underdog. Kindness and fairness mattered to me, even back then. I might have masked that side of me by acting tough, but when someone needed it, I truly cared. Years later, this was the side that Aaron Spelling saw in me when he cast me in *The Mod Squad.*

When it came to caring and friends, there was one special person I would really miss. She was beautiful, with long raven-black hair and olive skin. We weren't boyfriend/girlfriend, but we were very close. It was a kind of love—a spiritual connection and trust that drew me to her. She was Italian; her name was Marguerite Angela Madeline Macaluso, better known as Maggie. When I first met Maggie we were fourteen. She came from a religious Catholic family. She was a good girl who I found to be mysterious. We would sit at the beach or the park, and she would listen to my troubles, and more importantly, to my dreams. It was a connection I saw in her eyes that made me feel safe to be a dreamer. I could be vulnerable with Maggie. She understood.

As I sat there on the curb on State Street, thinking about my friends—Maggie, Faith, Ralph, Rappe, and Hanson—I realized even though I was leaving, this place was where my roots would always be. I remember sitting there, drunk, and taking one last huge swig from the bottle. Then everything went black.

It took two days for me to come out of the fog, and when I did, I found myself in jail wearing an orange jumpsuit that said "Dane County" on the back. I was told to shower, clean up, and put on my street clothes, which thankfully they had washed. Evidently when they found me I had passed out in the gutter. Ma had made the move to Milwaukee a few weeks earlier to get settled. Now she was coming back to get me, but not like how we'd planned. I was so ashamed.

I had to wait in the security booth with a phone so I could talk to her on the other side . . . when she showed up. I could see out into the hallway where the elevators were, and I waited for what seemed forever for her. I was afraid to see her because I knew how hurt she would be. When the elevator doors finally opened, I saw Ma and my Uncle Warren rushing to the desk to find me. I was so relieved that she had brought her brother-in-law with her and not Lorell. I couldn't have handled that.

When they finally let me out, Ma was really crying and I was too. Even the cops were touched by our reunion. I felt horrible that I had put her through this. Once we all calmed down and our hearts touched again, I promised her I was ready to accept going to Milwaukee and joining the family. I was trying to convince myself it wasn't going to be such a bad thing after all. I would be with Ma, and Ted would come home when he could. I would still have to deal with Lorell, but maybe things would be better now with my young sisters there.

Uncle Warren drove Ma back to Milwaukee. They agreed to let me stay in town for another couple of days to say my final good-byes. I had come to the realization that moving was the best thing for me. I was hoping that maybe life had something to offer in this new city. That is until I started thinking more and more about leaving one other person—Sharon.

Sharon and I had known each other for about a year. I know we were very young, but there was something between us from the start—stronger than anything I had ever experienced. The last night, before I was leaving Madison, we met on the steps of East High. I remember dragging it out for as long as we could. I remember walking her home, holding on to each other the entire way. I remember crying when we kissed good-bye. I was torn between wanting to stay with her and my promise to Ma.

The next day a friend drove me to Milwaukee. On our way out of town, I insisted we pass by Sharon's house. There she was—standing in the window, waving good-bye. I felt sick inside.

Once I was in Milwaukee, as hard as I tried, I'd find myself staring out the window in my room thinking of nothing else but Sharon. I'd listen to rhythm and blues by some of the greats: Johnny Ace, The Moonglows, Clyde McPhatter, B.B. King (I later became friends with him), Jimmy Reed, and John Lee Hooker. I didn't know how much of this I could take. I was so lonely and aching inside to be with Sharon. Ma realized that I wasn't myself. I was so unhappy. I even thought about suicide. It was in my gut. Ma and I would hold each other and pray that things would work out. It was one of those times when I turned to my buddy Christ. Otherwise my only comfort was the blues, and of course, the bottle. It must have been pretty obvious how I was feeling because even my stepfather was almost understanding in a way I had never seen him before.

I did my best to stay in school, and thought maybe, just maybe, I'd be able to make a new start, change my reputation and turn my grades around. At least Ma knew that. Milwaukee Washington was a tough school—very tough! I wasn't looking for trouble, but would you fucking believe it was right there in front of me? I was sitting at my desk, eyes half shut, trying to think. Evidently my foot was sticking out in the aisle a bit, and some bastard kicked my leg just to be a smart ass. I guess I had it coming as the new guy and all, but he had no idea about my emotional state of mind.

We met out in the hallway, and in no time flat I left him with blood on his locker after slamming his fucking head into it. This was the final straw. And then, as if things couldn't get any darker, when I was walking home from school I saw a young kid get hit by a car and killed.

It had only been a month—but I had to get out of Milwaukee and get back to Madison. The next day I got on a city bus, passing by the school and into downtown. From there I got on a Greyhound and left to go back to Madison. I knew Ma would be frantic, but

I had to go! I'd be sixteen in a few weeks and could finally legally quit school without anyone hassling me. Even my probation officer (who I was assigned to because of all the shit before) wouldn't be able to stop me.

When I arrived back in Madison, I stayed in a friend's garage so I could be close to Sharon. My friend's parents were very good to me. His mom's name was Lucille, and right away I thought of B.B. King's guitar. A couple of the guys gave me some clothes so I could at least clean up and look presentable.

The hardest part was calling Ma and convincing her that somehow this would all work out. Of course she was worried sick and I felt awful, but I just couldn't stay in Milwaukee. I made a few dollars from helping a friend clean his bar, and I kept out of trouble.

All I cared about was Sharon.

Chapter 2 - Sharon

In school there were these things called "slam books." They were small notebooks where each page had someone's name written at the top. The notebook would get passed around secretly in class to avoid the teacher seeing and confiscating it. Kids would write comments under each person's name, sometimes funny, mean, whatever they wanted. I remember one day it got passed to me and I saw under my name a remark that Sharon had written—"He's hot" or something like that. I got the sense she had a touch of the wild side too, which I liked.

I had noticed her many times before, but this ignited a switch in me. I know she could tell I was staring at her a lot, as she was me. She was beautiful, blonde, blue eyes, so pretty. She reminded me of an actress named Jean Peters. I finally got up the courage to be cool and approach her.

Hi, I'm Mick," I said.

"I know," she said. "I'm Sharon."

That was pretty much it. I had never felt the fire that combusted between us. I had girls who were friends—Maggie, Faith—but this was different. There is nothing like the first taste of passion. Teenage love and its intensity is undeniable. When I got back to Madison, we saw each other every night at different places. She would find some excuse to get out of her house and then we would meet. We were like crazy glue, bound together and holding on tight.

It didn't take long for word to get to her wealthy, influential parents that Sharon was with the bad boy, drinker, and dropout from the wrong side of the tracks. The more they tried to keep her away from me, the closer we got. The odds were stacked against us and that only made us more determined. We knew her family would never approve, but that didn't matter. Nothing mattered except being together.

The teenage/parent battle raged for many months until the inevitable happened. Sharon told me she was pregnant. We were two young kids, so inexperienced. I will never forget the fear in her eyes. I knew right then that we would get married. I would take care of her and our baby. I was sixteen years old, but I wanted this. I wanted to be a father, not run like the bastard who deserted Ma, Ted, and me.

I can still see us sitting in a dark stairwell at my friend's house, shaking as I called Ma.

"Ma, what would you think if Sharon and I got married?"

She responded, "Oh Mickey, you kids are way too young!"

Of course she was right, but I told her it might not be a question of age. I was frightened and happy in a strange and confusing way. We loved each other very much, but we were both very scared. We wanted to do what we felt was right and to us that meant having our baby.

We got married in Ma's apartment in Milwaukee. Ma, Lorell, and my sisters were there, which helped take the curse off. Ted was my best man. Thankfully Sharon's mother (a wonderful lady) was there too. Her father refused to come. Sharon looked beautiful. I was very proud she wanted to have our baby. After the small ceremony, Ted would drive us back to Madison. I remember we were sitting in the back seat of his car, and Sharon looked at me and simply said, "Thank you, Michael. I'm very happy." She was sixteen as well.

Still, I had a fear in my gut that her dad, who was a very wealthy and all-powerful man, might try and take the baby from us. I went to see a priest I trusted, and a guy I knew at the newspaper, and told them about the situation in case anything happened to me or to our baby. What was I afraid could happen? I wasn't sure, but I'd grown up in the streets. I knew I could end up with my ass in the bottom of a lake if things got real bad.

Sharon and I moved into a tiny apartment and within months, our daughter Candi was born—a mop top, beautiful little girl I adored instantly. I changed diapers, loved to feed her, put her down for her naps, and waited till she'd wake up again so I could hold her. Nothing could take her away from me. I had to support my new family and I was trying to find a job when a friend who was a meat cutter convinced me that I could get work at the Oscar Mayer plant of all places. Who would have thought the place I cursed as a kid would be where I ended up working? Well, on the first day of work I found out I had to join the butchers' union and I filled out all the papers. The next morning one of the union reps came up to me and said that I had a reputation for trouble so they were not letting me in. That meant I couldn't have the job. To this day, I have the feeling the real reason was that Sharon's father was behind this.

He gave me a job working at the bookstore he owned, where students got textbooks for their classes at the University of Wisconsin. (Someone told me that before I try and sell a book, I should read one first!) As much as I hated being under his thumb, it was a blessing in disguise. I was surrounded by books and students and suddenly I wanted to read, to learn - history, science, poetry. I also learned from the students who worked at the store part-time. This was a new crowd that I had never been exposed to and it was eye opening. I loved reading and discussing religion and philosophy. I also learned a lot from the classics. Thoreau was asked on his deathbed if he had made peace with God. He thought for a moment then answered, "I didn't know we had quarreled." That seemed to really fit me. The first sentence of Camus's *The Stranger*—"Mother died today"—has stayed with me for many, many years. At the same time, with all these new ideas roaming in my head, I was drinking more than ever and was again, living under someone else's complete control.

By now, Sharon and I were living in a really nice house. I was driving a new Oldsmobile, and had a couple of business suits (which I hated). But the deeper I got in this life that was created for us, the more I realized that none of it was because of me, and that didn't feel right. I knew I was supposed to be happy, but I wasn't. The house, the car, the suits, where did all this shit come from? I felt my father-in-law ruled my soul. If my soul had been for sale, I'm sure he would have bought it.

Sharon and I loved each other, but by now I was a full-blown alcoholic. Then Sharon was pregnant again, this time with our beautiful son Jeff. I loved both of our beautiful kids, but the marriage was in trouble. I was so emotionally screwed up, I don't know how Sharon put up with it for as long as she did. Things were just stacked up against us from the start and it all was falling apart. I had to leave. I moved from our house to a $6.00 room I could barely afford. Was history repeating itself? Was I like my bio father? That thought tormented me.

Sharon's older brother thought he was a tough guy and started following me around with his buddies. It was pseudo gangster shit, trying to intimidate me. With his dad's power he thought and acted like he was a little John Gotti. One night he and this buddy came over to where I was staying and said, "Let's go for a walk." Threatening me to keep away from Sharon. The street was dark. My buddies saw what was going down, and I could hear them jumping over fences behind houses to lend a hand if I needed it. Her brother heard them too and took off.

It was the last straw. I couldn't live under the watchful eye of her family. The more they pushed, the harder I pushed back. It was a combination of alcohol mixed with rebellion . . . on the rocks! Finally, I said, "fuck it!" It was inevitable. We were divorced by the time I was twenty.

The loneliest walk I ever took was when I left the divorce court after everything was taken away. Everything. It wasn't really mine anyway (except for the huge piece of my heart left with those two kids). I was down and out. I slept in used-car lots for the first of what would be many more nights. My bedroom was the back of old Buicks and Cadillacs that happened to be left unlocked. When it would get down to ten or twenty below zero, I thought I would freeze in the backseat of those old cars, but somehow I survived. Thank God my buddy had given me a coat because that's all I had to keep me warm. At least the snow was off of me and if I was lucky, the radio would work and I could fall asleep listening to old blues songs through the static AM stations.

Several months later, Sharon began dating someone. He showed up at the bookstore being a tough guy and wanted me to give him the six dollars I owed for child support. I was so broke I had to borrow that, but I did it because it was the right thing to do. I put my hand out to shake on the deal and he left my hand hanging out there with no response. I was humiliated and totally broken. I could have called a few of my old friends to kick his ass, but figured it wasn't worth it. If he got his ass kicked it would only be more trouble for me. Plus I needed to stop all the fighting and drinking and just move on. I knew in my heart that Sharon was a great mother and worked her ass off to see that all was well for the kids. At least I didn't fuck that up.

Now I had absolutely nothing. At one point I remember the beautiful Madison Capitol lights flickering across the lake, not too far from where Otis Redding's plane went down. I looked over and realized I was standing next to my ex-father-in-law's bank. He had won.

Across that lake I knew I had the one person I could always count on. I had some change on me so I dialed the pay phone.

"Maggie, is that you?"

Her voice warmed me right up. It was good to get some advice and support from someone who understood all that I was feeling. We talked as long as I could while shivering in the cold.

Maggie said, "You just keep going, Michael, and you'll be safe."

Sleeping in cars was getting old and wasn't always reliable so I started riding city buses all night. I got to know the drivers real well and if they were feeling generous, they would let me lie down in the last seat by the back window where I could fall asleep until the end of the route. The bus motors under the back seats kept me warm. On one of those bus naps, I dreamt of seeing a postcard with a picture of a child kneeling and praying by his bed. The walls of the room behind him were bombed out. He was obviously surrounded by the ravages of war. I had no idea where he was in the world, but somehow I knew this young person. He was alone. Maybe his bed reminded me of Ted's bed, the one we had to sell for a dime. Maybe it was me and my ravaged heart. I read the prayers of Kierkegaard to try and find some clarity. I finally came to the realization that I had to leave Madison and all I knew behind me.

Alone. Loneliness.

My only companion.

Chapter 3 – Summer of Love

To say I needed a change was an understatement. I knew I would miss my hometown, but things had gone from bad to worse after my divorce. I loved every chance I had to see my kids, but my relationship with Sharon was strained. I hated knowing she was with someone new. I realized that as difficult as it would be, the best thing was for me to go somewhere else. I was looking for some kind of sign to show me what my path in life would be. I still had the dreams and aspirations - the ones I had shared with Maggie, and I knew Madison was not the place to make them come true. Maybe they were just dreams, but if I didn't try now, while I was young and pissed at everything, I may never do it.

I was twenty-one when I joined one of my buddies, Dave, and headed to San Francisco. I had some friends who had talked about how great it was there, and I decided to give it a shot. I had nothing to lose. Everything about the city sounded intriguing to me. When I finally arrived I could see what all the talk was about. San Francisco is a state of mind. More than a city, it's an atmosphere. For the first time in years I didn't worry about anything. I met so many young people who were doing the same thing I was, looking for creative adventure and opportunity. It was like being with my buddies back on State Street, but on a grander scale. There was always somebody around to give you a joint or a sandwich or a floor to sleep on. During the 1960s, there truly was a love-in there. To paraphrase the great Scott McKenzie's song—if you're going to San Francisco be sure to wear a flower in your hair. That was the vibe all around the city and it was beautiful. Dave and I would go to art galleries. We wandered Golden Gate Park, Giradelli Square, North Beach and the zoo. We'd see young people sitting on the grass playing guitars and singing…beatniks. Peace and love. Everyone helped each other out. It was easy to make friends with people who lived like we did, from day to day. There were times when I even lived off the kindness of local prostitutes. It's the only time in my life that I've ever been stone-cold broke, basically alone, and I didn't care. It wasn't about money and material things; it was about meeting different kinds of people, and learning to open your mind.

One of the things I loved was that San Francisco seemed to have all four seasons in one day. It was an exciting change from the long winters that I was used to in Madison. Despite the kindness in the air, there were many occasions where I'd find myself starving. It goes with the territory of freedom, I suppose. Sometimes, when I was hungry and broke, I'd go to bookstores and flip through the mouth-watering cookbooks. If I could have, I would have eaten the fucking pages. At least it distracted me enough to take my mind off the hunger pangs for a while.

Living in the Haight area was magical. You could go to local places like City Lights Bookstore and run into the likes of Bob Dylan or Alan Ginsberg. I loved everything about it, but survival was always on my mind. Dave and I came up with a way to occasionally get a free meal. We would befriend a guy who we'd met at a bar and he'd invite us back to his place. Sure, he probably had other things on his mind, but we were desperate. If the guy said he lived on the first or second floor we'd go home with him, get drunk, grab something to eat, and then, before any sexual situation arose, my buddy would run off to the bathroom, climb out the window and jump down to the alley. After a few minutes, when he didn't return, I'd say "I'd better go see what happened to him!" and then jump out the window myself. Those weren't my proudest moments, but it was a matter of living from one day to the next. It was all about gathering experiences.

I think because there was such an accepting and spiritual atmosphere, I became more philosophical about things, and about life in general. I started to talk and sing to myself, letting my imagination take me to new places. I remember walking down by the docks and watching little whirlpools swirl at night in the wind when suddenly they were in front of me, getting bigger like a water spout, but it was just dirt and leaves. I even started to talk to the damn thing! I asked it what I should do with the voices I was hearing. I started writing things down and stuffing them into the pockets of old dirty jeans that are long gone, somewhere in the beautiful past.

Still, shit follows you and I found that out quick enough. Wherever you go, there you are, or almost there anyway. As good as San Francisco was, I couldn't escape being homesick, missing my kids, and yearning for what had been. You can't imagine how horrified I was when I received papers from Sharon asking me to turn over custody of the children so her new husband could adopt them. I guess in the back of my mind I saw it coming, but it was still a shock. I realized that I couldn't erase my past and I had to deal with it. I needed to think about what was best for everyone, and as hard as that decision was, I knew what I had to do. I signed the damn papers.

I didn't want what had happened to me and my brother to happen to my kids. I wanted them to have a father in their life every day, something I did not have, and this was the only way that would work. Even if I did go back to Madison, I would have to share custody and take them back and forth between homes. I didn't want that for those innocent children. I wanted them to have more, and I knew Sharon would make sure of that. Logically it was the right thing to do, but it hurt deeply. It was part of my responsibility of loving them. I was tormented by the overpowering urge to hold Candi and Jeff one last time. I was pissed off and hurt by the choices of my past, but there was little I could do. In time I learned to trust my decision, but it was always painful.

I was frightened and alone in a world that suddenly seemed dark and cold. I was lost, searching for direction and meaning in my life. It was around that time, I met a guy who worked the lighting for many of the theater productions at the University of California at Berkeley. He was another of the many gay men that lived in the city, and he was very kind. He knew I just needed a place to stay and he allowed me to live at his place for free. He did his thing and I did mine . . . and I never felt the need to jump out the window.

Once in a while, he would ask me to go with him when he was setting up the lights for an upcoming production. I was glad to help, plus I was curious about the theater. He would ask me to stand in certain places on the stage so that he could arrange and test the lights for an upcoming show. Every time I walked out on the stage I got a rush like I'd never experienced before. I could feel the energy even in the empty theater. I got chills imagining the audience watching my every move and it felt so natural to me. He would talk about what he was doing and try to explain how the lighting worked, but I was barely listening. I just felt like maybe I had found what I'd been looking for, or it had found me. You know what? I think I needed the attention. And this was the perfect way to get that. The audience would be part of my new family.

I had shared those dreams with Maggie long ago about one day acting and pursuing my passion, but I'd never imagined a place like this. I'd always told her, in that idyllic teenage way, that all I truly wanted was to be an actor, drive a convertible, have a daughter, and get an Irish setter. The experience of being on a stage made me want more, but I was broke and I needed to work.

I got a phone call from a friend living in Vegas who told me to come out there and he could get me a job as a bartender. I felt this as God stuff. Turns out there were four or five of my friends from Madison now working in Vegas. They would help each other find jobs. The only thing was that I'd never been behind a bar, although I'd definitely been under plenty. I explained to my roommate that there was work waiting for me if I could get to Vegas. He was kind enough to lend me fifty dollars for bus fare. Even after I left, we stayed in touch and kept up our friendship.

Vegas was a totally different vibe from San Francisco. It was nonstop day and night! There aren't even clocks in the casinos. I couldn't believe all of the cocktail waitresses. How could they look like that, be built like that, and bring you booze at the same time? It seemed too perfect, and of course it was. It was fantasy. It was also a drinking town, and I had been practicing that talent since I was twelve years old.

It was the era of the "Rat Pack" days, and the gangsters ran the town. Once I arrived, I was quickly offered a job at the Thunderbird Hotel, easily one of the hottest places on the strip at the time. I was told that I was the youngest bartender in the union. They didn't care anything about my past. (Hell, a lot of them had done hard time), unlike those bastards at Oscar Mayer. Most importantly I got along with all of the "bosses." And they were bosses in every sense of the word. I started to learn the ways of the town, to show respect to those running the show, and to keep my mouth shut. Every once in a while a colleague "couldn't" show up at work, and I later found out it was because someone had paid him a visit. Like I said, I learned not to ask too many questions because there was a term called "gardening in the desert." That meant that if you pissed off the wrong people, you might end up covered in sand, never to be heard from again.

I learned how to bartend and realized that it was a skill that would always come in handy. People are always going to drink. I could personally attest to that, so it made sense that I might as well make a living from it. Naturally I made friends with lots of people who worked in the bars, hotels, and casinos. It seemed like a place that was made for me and my hard-drinking ways. Here, I fit right in with the regulars and tourists who drank their way around the town twenty-four hours a day. I worked at Big Joe's Oyster Bar at the Thunderbird Hotel, one of the big ones on the Vegas strip. Joe's was located directly off the casino and was always busy. Lots of big name entertainers would stop by when they were in town, but the only autograph I ever asked for was from Bobby Darin. We struck up a conversation, and Mr. Darin actually encouraged me to pursue my dreams. That's something I will never forget.

One afternoon when nobody was in the bar, I was washing glasses or something, when I looked up and damn! In walks Louis Armstrong. He was by himself and just wanted a bowl of fish stew before his show. We talked for about an hour and I can still hear that gravelly voice in my head. He was as pure as the fresh-driven show. He truly was an ambassador to the world.

There was a well-known singing group called The Modernaires, who were frequent headliners at the Sahara. They were famous for their collaborations with Glenn Miller, as well as with the great saxophonist Tex Beneke, and the singing talent of Paula Kelly Senior. The music was the "big band" sound—not my kind of thing, but they were hugely popular in Vegas and toured all over the world. They even had their own television show for a while. One of my female friends worked behind the cash-out window at the casino. I dropped by to see her after work, and as gamblers were turning in their chips for cash we started talking. She mentioned that she had just met Paula Kelly's beautiful daughter, Paula Kelly Jr. "Let me introduce you," she said. "I think you'll really like her."

I was never one to turn down a drink or a pretty lady, so I figured why not. Here I was in a town full of life, and I was lonely as hell. When I met Paula Jr. there was an instant attraction. She was all of eighteen years old, stunning, sexy, and glamorous in her long sequined gown, done up to the nines.

Here I was, a bar boy, hanging out with this fancy woman and her famous parents. We dated when she was in town and had a great time together, although it was tumultuous from the start. She wanted my undivided attention and I was far from ready for any type of commitment. That led to jealousy, fighting, and way too much drinking. Besides when "The Mods" (how coincidental that name would become years later) weren't touring, Paula lived in Los Angeles. That created big problems because it didn't allow us much time together and made it hard to have any kind of relationship.

I often hung out with my coworkers after hours, many of whom just happened to be cocktail waitresses. One in particular became a good friend. Her name was Dee Dee. She had a wealthy boyfriend who I knew had recently bought a new house. One night she invited me to come over to see it. It was an amazing place. One thing led to another and we started making out. Things were getting pretty hot and heavy when all of a sudden we heard tires screeching in the driveway. I'll never forget Dee Dee's face when she looked out the window to see her boyfriend pulling up in his big ugly Cadillac. She screamed, "Shit!" Instinctively, I dashed into the bathroom, half-dressed and found myself once again jumping out of another window. This was becoming a way of life. Maybe it was time for another change. As I ran across the arid desert landscape I heard the click of a shotgun and a loud bam! That's when I knew my instincts were right. It was time to leave Las Vegas, and that's exactly what I did.

I heard the voice that told me what to do next. I think everybody needs a little help after Vegas (and not just in the form of a loan). I was in a state of *who the hell knows what's gonna happen now?* But somehow I sensed that I did have a plan. In fact, I didn't doubt it at all. I was going to find out where in this big world I belonged. Like Maggie told me before I left Madison, "Just keep going, Michael, and you'll find it. You'll be safe."

I hitchhiked to California and my ride dropped me off at a place called Point Mugu. It's a place I still visit to this day. It is part of a naval station just north of Malibu, on the Pacific Coast Highway. It was quiet and I sat nestled in the rocks and stared out into the vast ocean. At that time of day, late afternoon, the sunlight was traveling across the water. It was almost directly west. I could feel it soaking into my being. I heard it talking to me, trying to tell me something through the waves crashing on the beach below. I felt a sense of calm, of well-being, that I hadn't felt for a long time. Then the whispered voice of the elements came through: "Soon, Michael, soon."

I made my way down the coast to Hollywood. I got there about midnight. My luggage was a cardboard box with all of my worldly possessions in it: a Green Bay Packers jacket, two pairs of jeans, a few books of poetry, and a bible Ma gave me in 1954 which has never been away from my side to this day. There was a light rain, but I really didn't care. I don't know what I expected, but it damn sure wasn't this. Neon lights, people passed out in door fronts, a few gay hookers—it wasn't the glamorous place I'd heard about. I found the famous Hollywood and Vine intersection. With nowhere to go and no one to call, I wound up sleeping under the freeway overpass at Sunset Boulevard. The filling station on the corner was my bathroom. It was all about survival. (You know those sanitation cakes in gas station toilets? Take one of those, don't unwrap it, and put it in your back pocket. It keeps the bugs away!)

I hung around Hollywood trying to find a job. Thank God I had learned to be a good bartender in Vegas. It didn't take me too long to land a bartending gig at a popular gay joint across from the famous Huntington Hartford Theatre. It was called "The Office." Often members of the cast from the current play would wander over late at night to drink, unwind, and socialize. I found myself right in the midst of actors doing exactly what I had been dreaming of for so many years. I was so close that I could practically taste it!

It wasn't long before Paula and I reconnected. We were glad to be living in the same city. I didn't have a place to crash yet and would often sleep in the backyard of her family's house. As you can imagine, her mom and dad did not welcome the idea of a bartender and wanna-be actor camping out in their backyard. I tried to explain to them that I had a dream. I told Paula's mother that I wanted to do plays just like Ingmar Bergman. I said that because I wanted to let her know I was serious and knew who the hell Ingmar Bergman was. I loved the movie *Wild Strawberries* that he directed; I wasn't planning on being a lightweight actor. I knew what I wanted to do. Richard Burton, Paul Newman, that's where I was setting my goals. It seemed to impress her mom.

One night at the bar this theatre producer guy comes in. He'd been in several other times, and we struck up a conversation. I told him I wanted to be an actor, and he says he could give me a job. It would basically be as an extra carrying a spear. I'd heard a lot of talk about Hollywood deals and knew better than to believe or trust this could be anything other than drunken nothingness.

"So if you want to be a spear carrier, that's up to you. But if you really want to be an actor and you don't want to be a bartender for the rest of your life, you've got to find an acting coach. You've got to study!" Then he mentioned a name to me. "You should try to meet with Estelle Harman."

I asked around and found out that Estelle Harman had been the head of the UCLA Drama Department. She then went on to be Universal Studio's Head of Talent. After that she started her own actors' workshop where she was training actors, many of whom had gone on to great success. It was considered one of the best workshops in town. I didn't know if she would even talk to me, but I was young and brash so I went to see her and told her about the producer who had given me her name.

I wasn't sure what to expect, but what I found was a warm, intelligent woman who was very dedicated to the art of acting. She handed me a scene to read. It was the first time I'd ever done anything like that and I was nervous but excited. This was my chance! I had listened to the voices, followed the signs, and everything led to this moment. I read the scene as best I could. It was from the play *All My Sons* by Arthur Miller. It was the scene where my character talks about his dad building planes during the war that turned out to be defective, killing many innocent soldiers. It was very intense. Estelle read with me and when I was finished, I looked up at her, waiting for a reaction.

All she said was, "I want you to come back."

Chapter 4 - Estelle

Once I signed on with Estelle and her prestigious acting school, I was immediately immersed in the art that I had dreamed of as a kid back in Madison. I started out performing monologues from plays and films. I loved Dylan Thomas's "A Child's Christmas in Wales." I can still hear it in my head to this day, running through my mind like a Welsh mountain stream. "One Christmas was so much like another I can never remember whether it snowed for six days and six nights when I was twelve. Or whether it snowed for twelve days and twelve nights when I was six!" I also did "Dylan Thomas in America" where he explains to a child the mystical story behind "Baa Baa Black Sheep."

Estelle was a very astute woman and an excellent guide. She never tried to "teach" me. Her technique for me was to nurture the feelings that were already there and mold them to the lines and the character I was playing. If she had been heavy handed with me, that old script of battling authority would have reared up again, and I would have bolted, with a big "fuck you"! Thankfully Estelle had me figured out long before I did.

I worked as hard as I could in class. I was there to follow my dream and I wasn't going to waste this chance to make something of my life. I felt like many of the others seemed to be coasting along. Their approach was more academic than mine. I was serious, I was headstrong, and I was determined. I preferred doing long monologues from writers like Tennessee Williams by myself because I couldn't find anyone to match the intensity I wanted on stage. They didn't have the same manic energy. I figured, what the hell, I'll just do it alone. Eventually I started making friends with a few students and did some plays. One guy in particular, Jack Kelly, went on to great success. He starred in the TV show

Bret Maverick. I was happy for him when he became more and more successful.

For the most part, though, I felt that many of the students were more interested in being famous and rich than in acting for its sake. Money and notoriety were the last things on my mind. I just wanted to act. It wasn't even a choice! If I could master my art, I felt certain everything else would fall into place.

Alumni like Martin Landau would come by Estelle's to perform a small piece or talk with the students. I soaked up as much knowledge as I could. It sparked my passion.

One of my first actual performances at the workshop was the play *Luther* written by John Osborne. The play focuses on Martin Luther, a monk in the sixteenth century who basically said fuck you to the Roman Catholic Church. The play is very intense and focuses on Luther's rebellion and resolve to speak his mind even under the risk of excommunication. Needless to say, this was a role I could really relate to given what had happened to Ma and my battle with the church. I was onstage all by myself for two hours.

To prepare for the role, I asked a friend of mine to make me a robe out of an old cloth just like what Luther would have worn. I even built a little podium where I would give the speech about quitting the church. I was so intent on doing a good job that I wore that robe, sandals, and a big wooden cross hanging from my rope belt, walking to and from class and all over Hollywood Boulevard. That was my outfit for a few months while I rehearsed and performed that role. After the first performance, Estelle asked me if I'd do it for *all* of her classes. And, unbeknownst to me, she invited many of her casting director friends to see me. This was the first time I knew I could do something really well (other than drinking).

During this time, I continued to bartend part-time at The Office, where I met a gay couple who were regulars. We became good friends. They knew I was on my ass, so they invited me to stay in their spare room, no strings attached. I would come home from Estelle's at night and I would kneel by the bed with that robe on. They were so respectful of that and they never said anything to me about my odd clothes. They got it. They let me be Luther there and never questioned it. After a month or so I knew it was time to move on. I didn't want to take advantage of their kindness.

Estelle knew I was looking for a permanent place to stay and even more importantly didn't have the money to pay for one. She approached me one day. "You don't have a place to live, do you?" That's how I ended up sleeping in the prop bed on the stage at the workshop for about a year or so while I worked on my craft. We made an arrangement: I'd help around the place with whatever she needed, even wash her car, and she let me stay there. I was willing to do whatever it took. It wasn't always easy sleeping right there in the open. I'd get awakened occasionally by students who came in during off hours to rehearse. I'd stumble off to the bathroom and fall asleep by the toilet. It was a small price to pay for the privilege of staying at a place where I was convinced that I could make my dream a reality.

At first I thought to be a good actor somehow you had to be a professional liar. By that I mean you had to make somebody believe something that wasn't really true. Then Marlon Brando came along and changed the rules. I was in awe of his talent.

Stanislavsky's "method acting" became the standard for serious performers. It was basically an organic process of creativity that talented actors used, often unconsciously, to give a raw, real performance. Emotional recall came naturally to me. I found I could easily draw on my feelings and experiences of the past.

One of the famous schools of "the method" was the prestigious Lee Strasberg Actors Studio West. Lee was considered a guru of the method. A fellow student at Estelle's approached me about an audition she had for the Actor's Studio. This girl desperately wanted to study there, and I agreed to work with her. She chose a scene from *Picnic*, a wonderful play by William Inge. We rehearsed and rehearsed, and when the audition came, it went flawlessly. I could just feel how good it was. After we finished, we stood on stage in the dark waiting for some kind of reaction. There was silence. Dead silence. Finally a voice out of the darkness, one of the coaches, began to speak, but I stopped him.

"Why don't you turn the lights on so I can see who I'm talking to? Don't play fucking games where you sit out there in the dark hiding, while we're up here and supposed to be scared of what you're gonna say." Confront me, God dammit! My partner was shaking and I felt sorry for her (and by the way she was excellent), but at the same time I was frustrated and turned off by the whole process. The arrogance. I walked out.

Oddly enough, I got a call the next week, wanting to know if I was interested in becoming a member. They asked me to come back. I guess that was one time my rebellious nature worked for me. It was true though. I knew I was good at this and if they couldn't acknowledge it, I wasn't going to waste my time on them. Besides, I wanted to stay with Estelle. Acting with her was as natural for me as breathing. I trusted her with the emotions inside me, which were so available. Sometimes too available. I thought this ease I felt with acting must have been like how school was for Ted.

Not long after this, another of Estelle's students asked me to work with her on a scene. She had an audition at Paramount Studios for a movie and needed a partner. We got there that morning and performed the scene just as we had rehearsed so many times. I don't even remember being nervous. When we finished, one of the casting directors called her over and gave her the job right there! I was so proud of her and she was ecstatic. They walked off together to some office on the studio lot and I headed for the door.

Then the other casting director on the set yelled at me. "Michael, wait a minute. I want you to take this, study it, and come back at four to perform it. There will be someone here then who I want to see you." I looked down at the script he had handed me and figured, what the hell, so I raced back to Estelle's place and told her the news. She helped find me a partner to read with and gave us some coaching. We worked as hard as we could, watching the clock to make sure we allowed enough time to get back to the studio.

When I returned to Paramount that afternoon, I recognized Sterling Silliphant sitting in the corner talking with the casting guy. He was a handsome man with distinctive, silver hair. He could have been on either side of the camera. His reputation preceded him. He was a brilliant writer who had done a lot of TV work before moving on to screenwriting for major motion pictures like *Charley* and *The Poseidon Adventure*. He even won the Academy Award for *In the Heat of the Night.* He was a giant talent, and I was honored to be introduced to him.

Turns out he was developing a TV series based on the movie *Sunset Boulevard.* I wasn't aware that the casting guy from earlier that day had called Mr. Silliphant and told him that he needed to see me. He thought I was perfect for the lead, the role of Joe Gillis played by William Holden in the film. This time, the character was a young guy on a motorcycle who comes down from San Francisco with a pack of scripts, trying to break into show biz. I would be that screenwriter who becomes a part of the insular world of a delusional movie actress (Gloria Swanson in the original).

After my partner and I did the scene, I looked anxiously at Mr. Silliphant. He walked over to me, smiled, and said, "I want to do this show with you." I couldn't believe it. My hands started to sweat. I usually didn't get nervous, but in front of such talent, I was. Just then the phone off to the side rings and someone yells over to us. Little did I know the casting director, Eddie Morris, had called Howard Koch, the President of Paramount Studios.

"Michael, there's a call for you."

Me? Who could that be? I don't know anyone here.

"Hello?"

"Michael, this is Howard Koch. I want to see you back in the studio tomorrow afternoon for a screen test."

I didn't know what to say. I was in shock. This was so much more than I ever could have imagined. It was happening so fast. In a matter of just a few hours I found out how quickly your life can change. As it turned out, the creative genius that he was, Mr. Silliphant clashed with CBS and the show never got made. Great artists are always dueling with someone or something. That's what art is - a dueling contest with the artist against the critics, other artists, or society.

Before I left the studio that day, a man came up and introduced himself as Sid Gold. He was tan and bald, and I couldn't help but notice his gold pinkie ring with the initials S.G. Somehow I knew he was an agent.

"Have you got a phone?" he asked. "I want to call you tomorrow."

Shit, I didn't even own a jacket!

"Why don't you come to my office tomorrow so we can talk?"

I agreed. What the hell?

I was so excited to tell Estelle the news. When I walked through the door, she was waiting with a smile plastered on her face. I started to tell her everything that had happened, but she already knew. The casting director had called to fill her in. I couldn't believe all of this happened in one afternoon: a lead in a series, a screen test for Howard Koch, an agent!

Estelle continued to help me learn more about acting, working in TV and film, and most importantly how to work with other people. I had to learn to get along with fellow actors in order to build a reputation and a career. When possible, she would come to the set when I was working. She would calmly explain a scene to me in a way I could understand, helping me to draw on emotional recall. I was finding that many TV directors didn't focus on that because they didn't have the time. Sometimes, the actor needed to make the changes if a scene wasn't working. I always had a little test. If I didn't remember exactly what happened in the scene, I knew it must be ok because that meant it was natural. I wasn't *thinking* about the words and lines.

In 1966 I got my first paying acting job and it earned me a Screen Actors Guild card, which is a true rite of passage for any actor. Not to mention, you need it to work in this business. I was cast on the TV show called *Gunsmoke*. The episode was directed by Mark Rydell who went on to helm many movies like *On Golden Pond* and *The Rose*. It was the first episode of the first year that the show was shot in full color. Previously it had been in black-and-white only.

This was Mark's first directing job and I was asked to come in and read for the part of a character named Kip. He was a bad guy, basically a lying little bastard. Guess they thought I was perfect for the role! At the end of the show, the hero, Sheriff Marshall Dillon (James Arness), arrests me and takes me to jail. He wasn't playing around either. When we got to the cell, he threw me across the room like a sack of potatoes and I loved it! I knew I was "home."

Speaking of home, I heard there was a write-up in the Madison newspaper about a local boy who was going to be on network TV. It was accompanied by a small picture of me. I couldn't help but feel a sense of satisfaction knowing that everyone who thought I would never amount to anything would see that I proved them wrong!

That old saying, "be careful what you wish for" couldn't have been more appropriate. Things started moving very fast for me and my career. It was like a high-speed thrill ride and I had been dreaming of it my whole life. I got the lead in a film right after that! I couldn't believe my luck. It was called *The Bubble* and it was in 3-D which was the big craze in movies at the time.

Arch Oboler, the writer, director, and producer of the movie had helped to invent the 3-D technology that would be used on the film. He had remembered me from a play he had attended at Estelle's. This was my first movie role and I was excited to be working with an eccentric genius! Arch was a small guy, about five foot five inches tall, with thick glasses. He always wore a jumpsuit and a pith helmet. He was good friends with Russian composer Igor Stravinsky. He also had the habit of walking around with a couple of rocks in his pocket that he would click together as he talked. One day I asked, "What exactly are those?" pointing to the rocks he had pulled out of his pocket. "Those are meteorites," he said and walked away. Regardless of his eccentricities, I learned so much from him about moviemaking.

There was a huge premier for the film in Chicago. I couldn't attend the opening, but I was determined to go to the theater and see my name on the marquee. I made the trip with my costar, Deborah Walley (later known for the *Gidget* movies). When I looked up at the Woods Theater in downtown Chicago and saw the words "Arch Oboler's The Bubble with Michael Cole" it was a turning point for me and my career. It started to really sink in. It wasn't just make-believe. It was real! It was also the first time that people started recognizing me on the street as the same person they saw on the screen. That was a strange feeling that I never truly got used to.

I continued getting good parts on TV shows like *Run for Your Life,* a very popular action series starring Ben Gazzara. He was a consummate professional and I respected him. Another exciting job was being cast by Rod Taylor in a movie called *Chuka.* It was a Western and I was part of the cavalry, but I was a bad guy. I had committed treason and sentenced to death. I was shot by Sir John Mills and I died in Ernest Borgnine's arms! But before I was killed, I received a brutal lashing for my misconduct. That scene was captured in a book entitled *Lashings – The Top 100 Whippings Ever on Film*. Now that's a claim to fame!

By now, I was living with a buddy off Sunset Boulevard and Paula and I were dating off and on. As I got more and more acting jobs, she became increasingly insecure, straining what was already a fragile relationship. I had laser focus on my work and little time for anything or anyone else. That led to us breaking up.

During that split, I developed a relationship with a fellow actor at Estelle's. She was beautiful. In fact, she was the first runner-up in the Miss America pageant. She was also a great person and a damn good actress. We spent a lot of time together and I really liked being with her. It didn't take long before Paula heard about it, and she was devastated. I felt sorry for hurting her, and we eventually reconciled, but I had less and less time for her as the roles kept coming. Paula knew this was what I'd always dreamed of and she tried to be supportive. I explained it to her as plainly as I knew how. An artist doesn't have a choice; this is who I am.

About that time, I got a call from Sid.

"Michael, there's a role in a new TV show that is perfect for you."

I was intrigued. "What's it called?"

"I'll tell you when you get here. It's from a young hotshot producer named Aaron Spelling."

Chapter 5 – *The Mod Squad*

The next morning I went to Sid Gold's office to see what he had in mind for me. I was surprised to see little beads of perspiration forming on his shiny forehead, and I noticed the air condition-ing was on high. What's going on? He seemed to be getting very anxious. I was in my full James Dean/Brando mode at the time, so I figured he was anticipating my reaction to the premise of this new show he wanted me to audition for. It was something called *The Mod Squad*. He explained that the show was about three young people who helped the police solve cases. There was a street-smart guy, a troubled young woman, and a rebellious rich kid. He waited for my reaction.

"What bullshit," I said. "This sounds like the stupidest thing I've ever heard." Then I noticed even more sweat running down his sideburns and temples. "If you want me to audition, I'll be a bad guy. Give me a motorcycle or something, otherwise forget it."

"Michael," he pleaded with me. "Do me a favor, just go meet with Aaron Spelling. If you don't like what he has to say, you don't have to do it, ok?" And then he added, "Please don't fuck this up. Aaron is a very powerful producer."

He had a point, so I decided to give it a shot. I even borrowed a sports coat to look a bit more like a cop. Then I went to meet this guy that everyone seemed to be in awe of. When I walked into his office, Aaron got right into the pitch that I'm sure he had repeated many times as he worked out the concept. He started to tell me his vision of *The Mod Squad*, which featured three hippie undercover cops. "With their counterculture personas," he explained, "these kids can get into places where regular cops can't."

"Wait. . ." I interrupted, in my surly, cynical, rebellious way. "What kind of shit is that?" I want no part of harassing kids my own age, setting them up, arresting them, and getting them thrown in jail. Forget it!"

Aaron's eyes got big as saucers when he was excited, and the more I ranted and raved the bigger they got. I thought he was going to call security. I'd get dragged from his office and thrown out of the famous Paramount gates. Sid had to be thinking: This kid has the chance of a lifetime and he's killing himself. But instead of kicking me out, Aaron jumps up on his desk, and says, "That's exactly what I want! Exactly the attitude and the passion I'm looking for. You're it! You're Pete Cochran!"

"Yeah, well, I'm flattered," I said, but...."

Aaron was a very perceptive and persuasive guy. He said, "Michael, you've got it all wrong. It's not a cop show. It's not even about the situations the three of you get involved with. It's actually about the relationships among the three of you. It's about caring. The themes we will deal with will be handled differently than any other cop show ever on television. Nobody in *The Mod Squad* is ever going to arrest kids or turn them over to the cops or carry a gun, or even use one." I listened to this and started to believe Aaron's sincerity. When he put it like that, what could I say?

From what I understand, I was the first person to be officially cast in *The Mod Squad*. The show was still all over the place when I auditioned, but I knew it was getting down to the wire. I knew Aaron wanted me, but ABC feared I was "too actor studio-ish."

I was sitting in Sid's office a couple of weeks later when Sid got a call. It was Danny Thomas, Aaron's partner. Sid handed me the phone and I heard Danny say, "Hello, STAR!" Just like that! I got the job. I learned later that Marlo Thomas, Danny's daughter, who was filming her own show, *That Girl*, at the time, saw my screen test and told her dad, "That's your Pete!" Thank you, Marlo!

If I'd have said to Aaron I thought the idea for the show was beautiful, profound, and kids would go crazy for it, Aaron would have said, "Next." I was the right guy in the right place at the right time. And to think this had all happened in a few days too. Man, did shit ever change after that.

It wasn't only talent and my wise-ass big mouth that landed me the role of Pete Cochran. It was also luck. There are so many talented people in Hollywood, but very few ever "make it," or even get the chance. Luck is not a bad thing, but I believe there's a spiritual component involved in this too. Maybe luck and the spirit are the same thing in the end, like parallel lines that touch at infinity. You just have to know when the time is right. The key is sensing that what you're doing is something you need to do. Trust your instincts. This is the right place, and you're supposed to be right where you are. God put you there.

I remember the day I walked into Aaron's office to meet Clarence for the first time. I was nervous. I'd heard about him at Estelle's class. Clarence had been nominated for a Tony Award for *Slow Dance on the Killing Ground* so his reputation preceded him. Aaron introduced us. "This is Clarence Williams III." We shook hands, clasping one over the other as Aaron looked on, smiling. We were now two-thirds of *The Mod Squad*. Aaron's instincts were spot on. He had the uncanny ability to sense what would work for a TV show. He had an intuitive sense of chemistry. He knew that the right mix would be critical, and that we had to bond flawlessly for the show to work.

Aaron and the producers had already met with Peggy Lipton and wanted her to play Julie Barnes, but she hadn't been cast yet. They were having problems tracking her down. The story was that she was going out with Paul McCartney. I thought to myself that one of The Beatles shouldn't be too hard to find, but apparently he was, or at least she was. They eventually tracked her down in San Francisco. Robert Evans, president of Paramount, had her under contract at that time, so Aaron had to skillfully remove her from that obligation with contractual tweezers. Peg came across as very vulnerable when I first met her, but I could also tell there was much more to her. She was smart and business savvy! That came in handy when we all wanted raises!

The first day the three of us were together is one of my fondest memories. We were getting ready to begin shooting the pilot. Clarence and I were staying at a hotel on Sunset Boulevard. We were standing under the awning out front waiting for a studio car to pick us up. It was pouring rain, nobody on the streets, no cars, no vehicles whatsoever, and all of a sudden I heard this whine coming down

Sunset. I look at Clarence and say, "Damn, that's a nice little car." It was a red Porsche and the first thing that comes to my mind? James Dean. This car zooms toward us and then slides sideways on the wet street, parking perfectly in front of us. Inside the little red spider-like Porsche convertible is Peggy.

"Come on you guys!" she says. So I climbed into the back and Clarence, who is a lot taller than I am, got in the front so he could fit his knees in, and we took off.

As I said, this was the first day we were going to work on the pilot. Just as we got on the road, Peggy reaches down in her bag, right by the gear shift, grabs a rolling paper and some grass, and rolls a perfect joint with one hand, while shifting gears with her knee, and driving with the other. She just smoothly reached over and rolled the whole thing perfectly and coolly sealed it without even slowing down. Then she lit it and passed it around. That was the moment we truly became *The Mod Squad*.

But our trio couldn't do it alone. The fourth member of *The Mod Squad* was Tige Andrews, who played Police Captain Greer. Tige was a Broadway actor, the first guy to sing "Mack the Knife" on Broadway in *The Threepenny Opera* with Lotte Lenya.

Tige had great stories, and here's one that was a turning point in his acting career. While he was doing *Mr. Roberts* on Broadway, he noticed a scruffy, old, unshaven guy in the wings watching every performance. One night, Tige asked him if he wanted a seat.

"Thank you," the man said, "that's very nice of you."

One day, as they were talking, the older guy said to him, "Do you want to make a movie?"

Tige says, "What do you mean?" He's thinking this guy looks like he's just rolled out of the gutter, and he's talking about making movies? He must be crazy.

Just then he adds, "I think you'd be good as one of the lead guys." Turns out this raggedy old guy was the great director, John Ford. Being kind to Mr. Ford landed Tige a role in the movie version of *Mr. Roberts*, and the two of them remained friends until the end.

When Tige first came out to Hollywood, he did a show called *The Detectives* with Robert Taylor. It was another Aaron Spelling show, so Aaron knew he had that gruff quality to play Captain Greer on

The Mod Squad. But gruff and no-nonsense as he was, his character still had to have a soft spot for "the Squad." It was essential to establish Captain Greer's affection for the three of us, which was not shared by the chief of police. Tige's character had to walk the line between being hip enough to put up with us, to trust us so that we three respected him, and being "cop" enough for the police brass. He pulled it off perfectly!

The first week of shooting we were doing screen tests. Clarence and I were out somewhere, bouncing around Hollywood, buying a bunch of stuff—wardrobe and other things for the show—and signing Aaron's name for it. I said to Clarence, "All I have to do is learn to spell 'Spelling' and we can go anywhere in the world."

After all the contracts were signed and sealed, we were ready to go. The only problem was that Aaron didn't have an opening sequence for the show, "a teaser," and he desperately needed one. He got in his golf cart one day to explore the lot. Looking down a long alleyway, where old sets were stored, he found it. He shouted, "That's it! Water it down, make it look dark, and have the three of them running away from something in their lives."

That became the famous *Mod Squad* opening. When accompanied by that dramatic music from composer Earle Hagen, it set the perfect tone for the series. Were we running away from something or toward something? The truth is we were running from ourselves—that's the thought I used as an actor anyway. All I knew was that whatever was going on, I had to get away. Society! It wasn't for me.

We had hardly begun shooting when everything almost went up in smoke, literally! I heard on the radio that a huge fire had broken out at Paramount. I thought, we'd come this far, it's going to be a very successful show, it's got these great messages for people, and now the place burns down. Thankfully, that didn't happen.

I can only guess what people thought when they first heard the name of the show. "*The Mod Squad?* What's that?" In 1968 if you were a hippie, a radical, just a vaguely defiant young person, or even smoked dope, cops weren't your friend. Hell, I felt the same way myself. It would have made Abbie Hoffman's hair curl, if he'd ever heard of it, but by then he had shot his TV set, so he wouldn't have to ever look at Richard Nixon!

Just imagine you are a typical member of the television-consuming American public. It's fall, 1968. You've read about this new series, you turn on your TV, and there's *The Mod Squad*. What the hell could that be? They've put these two words together that don't belong. That's probably the reason half the people turned it on in the first place (and the other half turned it off). And from all the publicity they'd been bombarded with including the pictures of the three of us—a blonde woman, a black man, and a Mick (I'm as Irish as the Blarney Stone), we were going to raise a few eyebrows. Hippie cops. Get real! All right. Undercover.

Somebody had a cute idea for a show about counterculture cops, found three good-looking young actors to play them, and made up some hokey plots. That's what you'd think. Typical Hollywood exploitation, cashing in on the Pop Zeitgeist of the 1960s with a show about hippie cops who were going to bust kids who looked just like them. The idea of a show featuring a hippie sting trio, that alone seemed disturbing. You mean you could no longer identify undercover cops by their loafers and sweater vests?

I saw *The Mod Squad* as similar to the "family" portrayed in *Rebel Without a Cause* where James Dean (a loner, frustrated with his mother's emasculation of his father), Natalie Wood, and Sal Mineo (a shy kid who doesn't fit in), form their own family in an abandoned mansion. Our show was about young people from screwed-up families, who felt ignored and shunned by society, deeply hurt people who needed each other. In every show, we'd try to help someone in the same situation as the three of us—lost.

Our characters were each there for different reasons, each on the edge of delinquency, standing firm in our defiance of authority. We shared dysfunctional backgrounds. That's how we got together, and why we stayed together. Julie was a runaway, a flower child, her mom a prostitute. Linc was one of thirteen kids, had been arrested in the Watts riots. Pete was kicked out of his wealthy parents' Beverly Hills home, arrested, and on probation for racing and stealing a car. We created our own family, with Captain Greer functioning as our father figure, and we, by setting an example,

were rewriting the ethical issues of the culture. The campus dem-
onstrations, the anti-war riots, the drugs, the long hair—it was
those images in the headlines that were "threatening" to families
coming out of the 1950s bobby-socks mentality. We wanted to
establish that young people being portrayed in the news weren't as
bad as they were made out to be.

The Mod Squad changed the equation. We were a new breed
of "delinquent idealists." We had the space to deal with real-life
problems—ones our audience could connect and relate to. There
were story lines ranging from a disturbed soldier coming back from
Vietnam, to drugs, child abuse, and anti-Semitism. These were topics television had never touched! We were hitting on so many flash-
point issues that we got hate mail, some of it very extreme, almost
from the start. That let me know we were on the right track.

As a matter of fact, we were even told we'd made President Richard Nixon's enemies list. It was apparently a list of people who were
supposed enemies of that administration. Thousands of people
were on this list. Why were we on it? Because we cared about
young people, many who opposed the United States being in Vietnam. (Remember, the '60s mantra: Make love, not war!) One of the
producers said not to worry about it since we were all on it. Worry?
Shit! I was proud!

On the flip side, there were a surprising number of political people
who loved the show. I came to work one morning, and there were
helicopters circling over the Paramount lot. I thought it must be
for *Mission: Impossible* because it filmed right down the street from
us. Then I started noticing guys on the soundstage who were talking into their lapels. Man, this isn't *Mission*. I walked down to our
stage, and there were canvas-backed directors' chairs; one said "The
Governor" on it. Then one of the crew said, "There's somebody here
who wants to meet you." I walked over and found myself shaking
hands with Nelson Rockefeller, governor of the State of New York.

"Michael, I just wanted to come by and tell you how much my
family and I enjoy the show. It's an incredible job you guys are
doing." Holy cow, I couldn't wrap my brain around that one. I still
have a letter from him.

The Mod Squad was inherently groundbreaking regarding the issue of racism. From that very first freeze frame of the three of us clinging to each other—one black, one blonde, one white—that ran as a full-page ad in *The New York Times*, there was negative feedback. That image made people uncomfortable. It pushed a lot of buttons.

Clarence and I were very close and that genuine, loving friendship translated on screen. Sadly that didn't sit well with much of the American public at that time. In one episode Captain Greer got shot. Linc got his knife and was cutting around the bullet, trying to get it out. The camera shots they were doing were tight close-ups. Some sweat was going into Linc's eyes, and Pete reached in with a rag to wipe off his brow. The hate mail poured in! How could a white man wipe a black man's brow? Unbelievable! At the same time, from responses like this, I once again was certain we were on the right track.

In another example, when Julie gave Linc a friendly peck on the cheek, ABC, concerned that it would provoke a hostile public reaction, wanted Aaron to take it out. They told him, "You can't have a white girl kissing a black man." To Aaron's credit, he fought them and he prevailed. They warned him he'd receive thousands of complaint letters but he stuck to his guns.

Speaking of guns, in the beginning, ABC wanted us to use them. I refused. We didn't want to carry guns. I said, "What about all this shit? 'Hey, something's happening here,'" referring to Buffalo Springfield's song condemning police violence. "Can't you see there's a different mood in the country? We don't think the same way they do on *Dragnet*."

An important element in *The Mod Squad* was that it was as contemporary as the culture it mirrored. We were hip. Even our leader, Captain Greer, was hip—or at least he was working on it. When asked about the unlikely detectives he used on his force, he'd explain: "The times they are changing." "Uh, Captain Greer," we'd tell him, "that would be, the times they are a-changin'. Didn't we give you the Official Hippie Phrasebook to study? You gotta get with it, man. You gotta practice the lingo or you'll be like them. Repeat after me: 'dig it,' 'solid,' 'groovy.'"

The Mod Squad worked because it was in sync with the times. It was a kind of middle-school primer of the '60s zeitgeist. If it hadn't been "plugged in," it never would have been as successful as it was. We understood there was a line between what had been considered criminal in the past, and a new sensibility that acknowledged many of the old moral codes weren't working anymore. We always tried to find solutions that came from the heart. I had no problem identifying with these troubled kids; I was one.

As important as being in sync with the times, even more important was the chemistry among Peg, Clarence, and me. It was real. We loved each other. You can fake a lot of things, but you can't fake that. We never had one fight, one disagreement, or one bad word between us. In five years, not one. We always knew we could trust each other.

With the media mayhem and instant fame that *The Mod Squad* churned up, Clarence, Peggy, and I only had each other to turn to. We didn't even have to talk about it. It was self-explanatory. We comforted each other in a way that was the crux of the success of the show. At those critical moments, we needed each other and we came through for each other. Peg would get pretty upset and scared at times. We were on location somewhere and Peggy and I were sitting in the back of the car together. All of a sudden, she said, "Mick, can I lie down? I'm really beat." She lay down with her head in my lap. I stroked that beautiful hair of hers. At those moments, when she became scared, I would say, "It's ok, Peg. It's ok. We'll get through it fine." And right there, that connection with her went straight to my heart. This sealed the deal for me. A lot of people thought we should have had a romantic relationship on the show, but we didn't want to. Among the three of us, we had a relationship that was better than romance. I felt very protective of her. The relationships were very powerful and moving, they were magnetic, and they needed to be to get us through that onslaught.

The Mod Squad became so successful that it soon morphed into a cultural phenomenon. Our faces, the three of us especially, were like a pop Mount Rushmore. Once we went to see Sammy Davis Jr. in concert at the Los Angeles Sports Arena. He introduced us from the audience and called us up on stage. The noise was deafening, like a 747 taking off. The place was packed, you couldn't hear yourself think, never mind speak. Ringo Starr told me that in some of the places The Beatles played, they couldn't hear themselves over that liquid nitrogen wail of the fans, so they didn't even sing. They had become iconic, and no longer needed to perform—like Godlings, their mere presence sufficed. We were fast approaching a situation that felt the same to me.

At first, other actors were wary of appearing on our show. They thought it was too lightweight and silly. Once the show caught on, actors were asking to be guest stars. "Film actors" were even willing to come on the show, and back then it wasn't as common for a movie star to work in television. After five seasons, I am proud to say we wound up having eight Academy Award-winning actors as guest stars. A partial list of some of the great talent that appeared on *The Mod Squad* is: Ed Asner, Vincent Price, Andy Griffith, Richard Pryor, Lee Grant, Richard Dreyfus, Harrison Ford, Tom Bosley, Danny Thomas, Tyne Daly, Martin Sheen, Louis Gossett, Jr., Sugar Ray Robinson, and Rodolfo Hoyos Jr.

Sammy Davis Jr. did several episodes of the show. What had gotten him interested in the first place, and why he called Aaron, was because of a particular episode called "My, What a Pretty Bus" which was in the first season, the third episode. Each week, the three of us—Pete, Linc, and Julie—would inevitably get separated from each other, and then end up reunited. In that particular episode, I got separated from Julie and Linc and they were alarmed that I was missing. "Pete was last seen down at the docks." Ominous remarks like that. Then at the end of the episode I pulled up on a motorcycle. Julie and Linc ran toward me and we embraced. It was the first time ever on TV you see a white guy, a black guy, and a blonde girl in one shot hugging each other. It was a powerful image. That was the freeze frame. That picture went around the world.

Sammy told us he saw that episode and said, "I've gotta do this show." (He ended up doing two guest shots so he must have really liked it!) The first time he came to the set for his scenes I was nervous because I knew he'd be there. Sammy had his own wardrobe people and an entourage following him around. Before I got dressed, I walked over to the set to introduce myself. I saw his

Rolls-Royce in a specially marked parking place. (That's when you know you have a star around.) Sammy came running over and put his arms around me. He wasn't big, but he gave me a strong hug.

"Mr. Davis, it's an honor," I told him.

"Michael, no, it's Sammy!" There was that great smile! We became good friends from then on.

I'll never forget sitting in a dressing room and pinching myself as I listened to him talk. Here was one of the most talented entertainers who ever lived. He spoke in a rapid-fire flurry of hipsterisms, and could do uncanny impressions of other celebrities. Sammy was a big joker. All the guys in the "Rat Pack" were. He, Sinatra, and Dean Martin were always playing elaborate practical jokes on each other. So the crew thought they would play a prank on Sammy, and it was a doozy. They hid Sammy's Rolls-Royce. They drove it onto the lot, and during lunch the crew lifted his car high above the soundstage. At the end of the day, we're all going home, and Sammy comes running back in yelling, "Where the hell is my car?" He charged up to Aaron's office, ranting that someone had stolen his Rolls. Of course, Aaron knew what we had done, so when Sammy came in raging, he burst out laughing. When Sammy went back to the soundstage he said, "Ok, wise guys, where did you stash my car?" They pointed up. Sammy doubled over he laughed so hard, twirled around, and did a little dance. Sammy Davis Jr. was pure showbiz. He was somebody who could do a dozen different things brilliantly, and through sheer force of personality transcended being any one of them.

Chapter 6 – You Need a Break

Shooting a TV show can be tedious at times—waiting all day for your two-minute shot is boring as hell. Even if there was a special guest star that week, they would usually arrive just when their scene was scheduled to be shot. So out of boredom Clarence and I would fool around during downtime, between shots. For instance, we would show up on other people's sets. We'd go over to where they were shooting *Mannix*. Mike Connors would open the door of his trailer to run into the next scene, and there were *The Mod Squad* guys, standing there making silly remarks, as if we were part of the show. Like, "Hey, Mike, what's your hurry? Where you going? Let's go have a beer. We got some hookers lined up!"

We used a lot of motorcycles in *The Mod Squad*. I was a fairly good rider so I would take one out every once in a while and go for a ride when we were on location. Word got back to Aaron and he was very worried that I would do something crazy and crash, which would mean we would have to stop shooting, which in turn, would cost a hell of a lot of money. He didn't want that!

Well, one day on location during a lunch break, I took one of the bikes and had a great ride in the hills by Griffith Park. Only one thing was wrong—I didn't know Aaron had come to the location to see how it was going. I realized it was getting late and time to get back because I still had scenes to do. I didn't want to hold up the crew, so I really turned it on. I had no idea Aaron would be there waiting for me! I came screeching back, popped a wheelie, and skidded to a stop just outside my trailer door. Aaron heard the bike coming fast and dove into the trailer to get out of the way. He landed by the toilet. Oh shit. This was the producer and my boss! Neither of us was hurt, but was he pissed! I felt like an ass in front of the crew and guest actors.

What the hell would I have done if he had wound up *in* the toilet? It was amusing to me, but not so much to Aaron. Needless to say, that put an end to my joyriding for a while. I thought to myself, thank God I was one of the stars of this hit show so he couldn't exactly fire me. When he left, we all laughed like hell!

The crew and I once laughed so hard we practically split our sides. There was a scene set in the morgue. Pete and Linc were there to look at a body that had been burned. There was the gurney with a sheet over the body (played by one of our stunt guys). The coroner is warning us, "This is a gruesome sight. I don't know if you are ready for this." He starts to pull the sheet back and I hear this thud. Linc, who was always so stoic and tough, suddenly "fainted"! One look at CW on the floor and we both burst out laughing; the guy under the sheet starts laughing, making the sheet go and down. It took twenty minutes to resume shooting!

You need a laugh every so often to lighten things up from the hard work of shooting for days at a time. Cast and crew! I remember we were finishing shooting an episode that involved the circus. In one scene, there was a very pretty girl standing on an elephant that was lying on its side as she was washing it with a brush mop. The camera started out on the trunk and then panned down to get the entire beast. It was to circle the animal from trunk to back end to capture its enormity. I know the elephant didn't like what was going on around her. All these people, the equipment. So she waited as the camera started moving toward her hind end. Her timing was perfect! As the camera got within three feet of her ass, she farted! LOUDLY! The sound guy almost fell off his chair as he tore off his headset. The cameraman did fall off the dolly when the flapping ass crossed his lens. Then someone on the crew yelled out—"Man, that's the first critique of this episode!"

We were out of control for the rest of that day!

* * *

Not only did *we* need a break sometimes, so did Pete's famous car, The Woody, an old green 1950 Mercury station wagon with wooden panels on the sides. We drove The Woody for the first couple of years of the show and it became like one of the cast. However, it got stupid when this '50s-something Mercury station wagon was catching up to Lamborghinis in chase scenes. So we made a deal with Dodge and started using very fast Dodge convertibles on the show.

Even though we loved the old Woody, it was time to get rid of her. So the writers wrote her "a final scene" . . . she would be lost over a winding cliff road in the mountains outside Los Angeles. In the scene, the three of us are in the car, and I'm driving the old girl as fast as she'd go down a steep road. The brakes didn't work and we would soon be careening over the edge. The three of us bail out just in time. Of course, that's when the stunt guys took over to send her flying over the cliff.

Clarence, Peg, and I walked up the hill to watch our friend take her last breath. I think the whole crew felt bad. Anyway, here she comes down the dirt road as fast as she could, heading toward the cliff. The stunt people bail out and we all thought . . . there she goes! She rolled about fifteen more feet to the very edge of that cliff and stopped! What? The stunt guys were a little embarrassed, but they knew they had done their job perfectly. Ok! One more time. Everything's a go.

Here she comes again, maybe going a little faster. The stunt people bail out again and damn if the exact same thing didn't happen again. She rolled about ten feet and stopped just before the edge. This time everyone just stared at her. It was becoming clear she didn't want to go over that cliff. The stunt guys apologized, but we were all thinking the same thing. The old Woody just wasn't ready to go yet.

One more time! This time they would make it work. There were four cameras at different places to capture the whole thing. She was to go over the cliff, roll about five-ten times, and then catch on fire. The stunt people bailed out a third time.

Everybody, including me and Peg, were holding each other's hands. Well, she finally went over the side, however she would not roll. She just stopped about twenty feet down the steep embankment and sat there. I know her spirit was asking why we were doing this to her. She had served us mightily. Didn't we know that?

She was still about forty yards away from where she was supposed to crash and catch fire. The guys had to move her to the spot where the firemen had their equipment ready to put out the fire. We stood there watching and wondering what would happen next. They rigged an explosion and we cleared the area. ACTION! A small flame started and then she blew. But before the firemen could put her out, a strange thing happened. All of a sudden, as she was burning, from deep within, the horn started screaming. I know it was her soul leaving the body of The Woody!

All of us, the stunt people, the firemen, and the crew saluted her for battling as hard as she did. A tear came down my eye as we said good-bye to our old friend. I couldn't watch when she was hauled away.

Chapter 7 – Fame

Fame is being a crossword puzzle clue!
Fame is being an answer on *Jeopardy!*
Fame is being on the cover of *Mad Magazine!*
Fame is some crazy shit. Before you know it, weird things begin happening to you. With fame comes money, and when you have money you start buying stuff and the next thing you know people are trying to steal it from you, and if you're anything like me, you end up in your driveway, naked, shooting a gun at a complete stranger.

Unlike my two costars, Clarence Williams III and Peggy Lipton, I didn't understand fame. Even with a certain sense of shyness I had always felt I could walk into any situation—bar or otherwise—and handle it, but this was something else. When I walked into Paramount for that audition I just felt I belonged there. What happened next was impossible for any beginner to prepare for. Forget paying dues or what you thought might be dues. I didn't have a clue! At the start of the first promotional tour, the publicist told us, "Do you realize that your lives are never gonna be the same again?" I had no idea what she was talking about. Clarence had been a big star on Broadway, so he'd already been through it. And Peggy knew everyone in the world from Dean Martin to Frank Sinatra to Quincy Jones to the Cat in the Hat. But me, I had no frame of reference whatsoever. And *nothing* ever was the same again.

When we started making the pilot, I was still walking to work every day. I'll never forget one morning looking up to see a huge billboard of *The Mod Squad* on the corner of Melrose and Gower, at the Paramount building. There I was—twenty feet high! Seeing yourself on a giant billboard, it does something to you. Your molecules get rearranged. It's hard to readjust your mindset after that.

This was only a few blocks from where I used to sleep under the freeway.

The Mod Squad soon became the top show on TV and perhaps more importantly, a fixture in popular culture. And I, who had no idea who I was or what was starting to happen, was swept up in that pop tsunami.

There was all that money that came flying at me for the first time in my life. I was clueless about how to handle it, since I'd never had any. Thank God, Sid got me a business manager! Like I said, I was still walking to work. One day I was with a friend and we passed a car lot. There sat a beautiful James Dean Porsche. "Man," I said, "that is one pretty 'little bastard!'" It literally had "Little Bastard" on the license plate, and it was a Silver Porsche Spyder—one of only ninety in 1955. We got about a block away and my friend stopped me and said, "Michael . . . you know, you could have one of those." *Whoa!* I thought, *maybe I can.* It wasn't long before I was driving a little Porsche and eventually other sports cars. Not bad given that a few years prior I'd been sleeping in backseats of old sedans in a used-car lot in Madison.

If you're an artist and a dreamer and you suddenly experience success, and out of the blue people are giving you money and buying your talent—it's disorienting. You don't know where it came from and you ask, "Where were you when I was totally on my ass and having to use the 76 station for my bathroom?" Fame, money, it's all just on loan anyway. Be a star and have everything you think you want, but don't get too comfortable. That's my advice.

When you're poor, you don't know what money can do, but I was finding out real fast. After totaling my first couple of sports cars, I took my accountant's advice and bought a big solid piece of German steel, a four-door Mercedes sedan. What my agent actually had said to me was, "Enough with the Porsches and Jaguars. I want you to buy yourself a *tank*, otherwise meeting your idol James Dean might happen sooner that you anticipated." Aaron Spelling agreed.

It was a green Mercedes, green for the Irish Catholic in me, and I parked it in my driveway. Would you believe in less than a week some bastard broke into it and stole the radio? It was an expensive German Becker. It could happen to anyone, right? *Once.* Then it happened again. Ok, that's it; don't fuck with a guy from the wrong side of the tracks! I'm in bed, but my ears are like bat radar. At two AM, nothing; three AM, nothing. At four AM. I hear a pickup truck backing down my driveway. I jump out of bed naked, take my .45 out of the drawer, and run outside. I'm still a little drunk from the night before. I sneak around the side of the garage in time to see the truck door opening. I shout, "You fucker!" The guy turns around and sees a naked man with a gun. A man with a gun maybe you can reason with, but a naked man with a gun? Then I fire the gun in the air, and the neighbor's lights come on. The thwarted radio thief jumps in his pickup and peels out of the driveway, never to return. My next-door neighbor comes out on his balcony and sees me. I hear his wife in the background shouting, "What was it, hon?"

"Go back to sleep, it's nothing. Just Mickey shooting off a pistol naked in the middle of the road."

When the show took off, fans included people like Elvis Presley, Sammy Davis Jr., Dean Martin, and Steve McQueen. That was mind-boggling to me. Elvis was a fan of *mine!* The Rat Pack's seal of approval was like getting knighted by the queen. And Steve McQueen, he was the coolest of all, tearing up the hills of San Francisco in his Ford Mustang 390 GT Fastback! McQueen was the only guy I knew who drank rye, the same as my stepfather. I remember McQueen with fondness. He was totally his own man, did shit his way, or not at all. Hopefully I could learn something from him or some of the other guys I looked up to as this weird fame thing started to take hold of my life. To this day, it still catches me off guard when people I have never met know my name. Fame.

Since ratings for *Mod Squad* were good from the first season, it was a lot to handle for the guy everyone in Madison, Wisconsin, thought was a total loser. The sudden stardom was something that no one back home would ever have foreseen. Not in their wildest dreams did anybody think I would be run out of town, and then in just a few short years become a star on television. I have to admit, that was a great feeling. When the first *TV Guide* cover came out, *whoa!* That threw me for a loop. Not only was I on TVs all across America, I was on everyone's coffee table too!

Like I said, dealing with fame was not easy. At first I tried to be nice to everybody. It is flattering being recognized. But it didn't take long to get tired of the lack of privacy and cameras flashing in your face. That's when it dawned on me why they have so many private clubs in L.A., places where the "stars" could go and not be bothered.

The Daisy in Beverly Hills was such a place, and one of my favorite haunts. It was always packed with actors, models, and the "beautiful people." It was a party scene and a fun spot where I would hang out till the wee small hours of the morning. Another was the Rain Check Room on Melrose. It too was a hot place where you'd find actors, writers, directors, and the who's who in show business. I remember Shelley Winters coming in the night she won her Academy Award. She literally had her Oscar in one hand and a drink in the other. She was celebrating. Within ten minutes she was on the phone yelling at her agent about him not getting her any work.

Clarence and I hung out together often. He was going through the same experiences I was, but he handled it better. I was most comfortable with other actors or "bar regulars." I didn't care who I drank with. Clarence wasn't a dedicated drinker, so he would look after me. He knew after a few too many drinks I could go from relaxed to raging, and he would say, "Man, let's get outta here!" But it didn't stop me. Wherever I'd go, someone would pick up the tab. Can you imagine what that is like for an alcoholic? It hadn't been so long ago when all I could afford was an eighty-nine-cent bottle of rotgut called Silver Satin, the supposed inspiration for the song "Drinking Wine Spo-dee-o-dee." I think, "Where were you when I was drinking cheap wine, living under the freeway?"

So my drinking didn't slow down. I held it at bay when I was working. But after hours I was trouble. I got thrown in jail more than a few times for fighting and DUIs. I thank God I never hurt anyone when I drove. The cops must have had some sort of deal with the producers because Aaron would get a call when I was arrested.

"We got your boy down here."

"Is he all right?"

"Yeah, there was a little trouble last night, but he's fine."

Somebody from the studio would come over and get me.

One time a cop came by the holding cell I was in. He said, "You're great on the show, Michael. I feel kind of bad."

"That's ok," I said. "It's your job. I would rather be here than on Skid Row."

Then he says, rather embarrassed . . . "I gotta ask you a favor. My daughter would never forgive me if I didn't get an autographed photo from you." He put the photo through the bars of the cell and I signed it for him. "Thank you, man," the cop said. "We'll get you out of here soon as we can." And he did. I got back to Paramount, brushed my teeth, went to makeup, and went right back to work. That's what fame can do!

You could always tell the drinkers on the lot. They'd be the ones lined up at seven in the morning, outside the nurse's office, waiting for their B-12 shots. It worked, because after you had one of those you felt fine. It gives you energy, and counteracts the leftover alcohol in your bloodstream. So I always got a double. Despite the fact that I was a heavy drinker, working the next day was never a problem for me. Sometimes, if I knew there was an emotional scene coming up, I'd stay up all night and be wiped out the next day, which in its own contorted way, worked. If the scene was sensitive and emotional, I was so fucking raw that I was *there* emotionally. It was my own little method-y thing. After I'd done the scene I'd go to my dressing room and sleep. But the damn scene went beautifully, and that's all I really cared about.

Being recognized, and often getting harassed, became so commonplace that I started calling it "the old recco" which meant I was about to be recognized. And of course, because of my lifestyle, it happened a lot in bars. In fact, bars can become tinderboxes when you mix alcohol and fame. One time we were on location shooting an episode of *The Mod Squad* near Vegas. We wrapped early, so a buddy of mine, an aspiring actor and close friend, headed with me to the nearest bar. This was a small town, and it was a rough fucking little place. We were the only two guys in there, drinking Crown Royal, eighty-proof Canadian whiskey, and swapping stories. Then in walk four or five guys. These were tough guys.

The bar itself was circular—shaped like a crescent moon—so you're facing people on the opposite side. Sure as shit, one of these big guys looks up from the other end of the bar.

"Hey."

I'm trying to ignore him, but I can already see this isn't going to end well.

He says, "Hey, I'm talking to you. I know you. You're the one who works with that (*n-word*), ain't ya?"

I stood up. Inside my heart is pounding—bang, bang, bang, bang. I looked at Joe and we both knew we're about to get our asses kicked. Still no way would I put up with this shit.

"Yeah, I work with him. He's my fucking friend. Why?"

With that, a couple of his boys started to get up. I backed away from the bar because that's one of the first things you do when a fight is about to start. The beer bottles are on the bar so it makes sense to get the hell away from that glass. Just then, Ronnie Rondell, my stunt double, comes walking in with Glenn Wilder, and five other guys from *Stunts Unlimited*. Trust me, you don't mess with stuntmen. They see what's going down and slowly move in behind me.

Ronnie says, "Which one?"

I pointed, "That fucking guy right over there thinks he's pretty tough."

Ron slowly walks over to the guy and says, "Do you have a problem?"

Boy, did he change his tune fast. "No, we was just talking, talking about that show."

Ronnie looks at him and his group and says, "You better leave, NOW. I don't care if you've finished your drink or not. Get out!" One or two punches were thrown, but that was that. Thank God for Stunts Unlimited! Ronnie very probably saved my life. And it wouldn't be the last time! *Fame.*

One time in Dallas I was sitting at a bar, waiting for someone. My hair was pretty long then. This guy starts staring at me. Then it started.

"What do you think of John Wayne?"

What the fuck kind of question is that? I said, "I think he's one of the biggest stars in the world."

"Oh yeah, then why don't you cut your hair like his, you fuckin' hippie asshole?"

He was on his way over to get in my face when two beautiful ladies, maybe in their 60's, interrupted. They were very refined looking in their pearls, and obviously had no idea this guy coming over wanted to crush my skull. "Excuse us, Mr. Cole, would you mind giving us your autograph?"

I said, "Absolutely. What's your name?" I signed each one of their napkins and thanked them. They must have carried some weight around the restaurant because I saw the guy split. These two wonderful little ladies unknowingly had just saved my ass.

The angel who's watching out for me was probably asking himself, "What am I gonna do now? There's no stuntmen around to save his ass this time." Then he sees a couple of ladies, "Oh, those two will do just fine."

As I think about all this, fame—coupled with the insecurities from my early years—was the root of many of these situations. Someone would say, "Hey, I know you. I can't believe I'm sitting next to a fuckin' cee-leb-rit-tee!"

"Know something," I'd tell him, "me in a dump like this, and me at the Emmys is the same guy."

Fame can be scary.

I was very surprised when I started learning about all our dedicated fans. I loved them! To this day, I refer to them as my "friends." They were crazy about *The Mod Squad* and the three of us (and still are), but that exuberance is where the downside of fame would sometimes creep inside me. When we were out in public, their enthusiasm and excitement would often spin out of control. Sometimes people would reach out and grab at your clothes or your hair, all the while screaming hysterically. It was intense *Mod Squad* mania. That's when it got scary. The fact that this was going on right after Bobby Kennedy's assassination intensified that fear for me. An extremely excited and emotional crowd can be a frightening phenomenon, especially when you are in the middle of it . . . and you're the cause of it!

One time during hiatus, I went to New York to hang out with Clarence. We wound up at a huge, very famous disco late one night. We couldn't even get in the front door because there were too many people starting to recognize us and a crowd was forming. The owner of the club, with a couple of security guards, came and got us and brought us in up to the second floor via a fire escape. From there, we could look down on the dance floor and watch Sly and the Family Stone perform. Pretty soon, Sly looked up and waved, and with that, it was over. People turned and saw us, and that was it! We reached down to try and shake a couple of hands, but by then, it got crazy scary. There was pushing and shoving and it was quickly getting out of hand. I looked at Clarence and I said, "I'm outta here!" We made it out through the fire escape to the car. By then, the cops had blocked off the streets to make a path for us, but a group of kids somehow broke through the barriers and climbed up on top of the limo, pounding on the roof and screaming our names—their faces against the windows. It took the cops on horseback to clear the way so we could get out of there. It was sheer pandemonium.

Fame can be terrifying!

I was with a good buddy at the Daisy one night in 1968, and someone invited us to a big party at Roman and Sharon's. Let's go! The incredible director, Roman Polanski, was in town and the house was full of the rich and famous—Abigail Folger, Warren Beatty, James Colburn, Mama Cass Elliot. Talented, amazing people. The party was sprawling inside and outside. I was introduced to Roman, and to his beautiful wife, Sharon Tate, who was pregnant. My friend and I hung out and bullshitted with some other folks for a while. Then we took off.

One day later I hear on the radio that Sharon Tate, Abigail Folger, and three other people were *murdered* in that house where we had been the night before. I had to pull over when I heard the news I was so shaken. It was horrifying. I couldn't comprehend that I had been in the room where later the word "Pigs" had been scrawled on the wall in blood. It was reported later there was a hit list. People like Steve McQueen were on it. This town was terrified.

It was one of the times when fame was the last thing I wanted.

Fame makes things happen!

Some friends and I went to Hawaii to look at some land for a potential investment. I was staying at a beautiful hotel, The Royal Hawaiian, right on the white sands of Waikiki. As much as I just wanted to hang out and relax on the beach, the old "recco" was making it impossible for me to have any downtime without being approached by fans. Out of nowhere, a Samoan guy comes up to me and says, "Aloha, Mr. Cole. My name is Jesse. I have a place just down the beach for you and your people." Turns out he had roped off a private area of the beach for us. It was pretty cool. Jesse and I became friends, and he was also my bodyguard. Anything I wanted or needed Jess could get! The next time I went to Hawaii, I took Ma. Jesse was there to meet us and never left Ma's side.

Fame has its privileges!

At Christmas, it was wonderful to be able to buy gifts for Ma, and for friends. All I had to do was call several stores in Beverly Hills, and they arranged to have a personal shopper select a bunch of merchandise that was delivered to the studio so I could "shop." Clothes, jewelry, you name it. I would pick what I liked and for who, and they took care of everything else.

Fame can make you proud.

Like the time I was in Chicago and noticed Sammy Davis Jr. was playing there. I wanted to see him so I called the theater. When I got there, they asked me if I would wait a few moments so Sammy could go on. Shortly after his show started, I was escorted to a front row seat by a couple of security guards. Sammy told the audience that a special friend of his was there this evening. He gave me a beautiful introduction and brought me up on stage with a huge hug. The place went crazy! They stood and cheered. I was so honored—not to mention that my seat was next to Dr. King's people. That made me very proud!

Fame can open doors!

Dr. Martin Luther King's "I had a Dream" speech in 1963 - his words, his dignity inspired me. When he was assassinated in 1968, I was compelled to personally go to Atlanta to pay my respects, which I was able to do after the first season of The Mod Squad. Ted was living in Atlanta then, and we made the trip to Ebenezer Church together.

We got to the church late in the afternoon, only to discover it was closed. I knocked on the door anyway, and to my surprise, a beautiful, tiny African American lady cracked the door open, and when she looked up at me, I could see the recognition set in. She opened the door and let us in. It was just me and Ted, alone inside, but Dr. King's spirit went right through me. I wandered around eventually made my way up to the pulpit. It was so powerful to realize I was standing in the same place where he preached. I looked out to the congregation and saw the organ off to the side, that Coretta played. I couldn't help but shed some tears.

After that, I sat in a couple of the church pews to get a feeling for what it must have been like to be where the people sat. I picked up a hymnal and noticed there was a Spearmint gum wrapper marking the page and the hymn they sang. I thought about keeping it, but I knew I had to leave everything just as it was.

On our way out, we thanked the lady who had allowed us to come in. To this day, when I think of being there, it still brings a tear.

Or, the time in Las Vegas, when B.B. King introduced me and had me come up on the stage at the end of his show. Fans were screaming like hell. Afterward he invited me to his dressing room where I met his band. Believe it or not, B.B. was making everyone fried chicken in an electric frying pan. It was fucking GREAT! We talked until his next show. What a beautiful artist . . . and what a good cook!

Kathleen Hyland Cole. "If there are any heavens, my mother will, all by herself, have one." -e. e. cummings.

Me with my best friend and brother, Ted.

Ted, Ma, Nana, and me.

Ted, Ma, and me at Aunt Janie's house.

Ma, my sisters Colleen and Deborah, and my step-father, Lorell.

Gunsmoke - 1966 *The first year it was shot in color. Courtesy of CBS Broadcasting Inc.*

Aaron Spelling directing me and Clarence Williams III.

Me, Clarence, Sammy Davis Jr., and Peggy. I was so proud Sammy did the show twice!

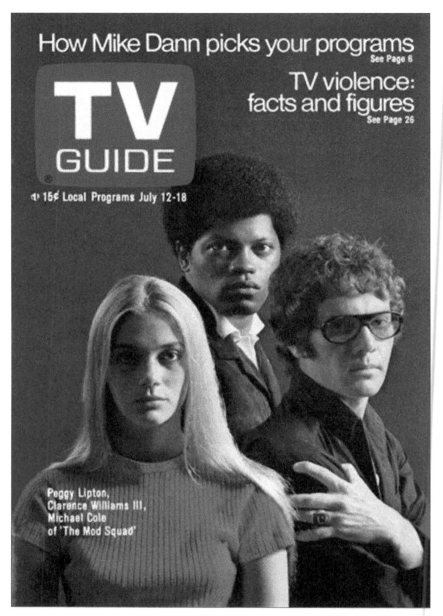

TV Guide. *Courtesy of Sai Saha,* TV Guide Magazine.

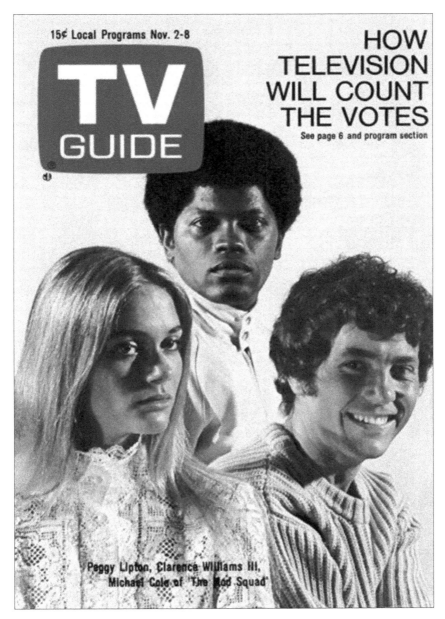

TV Guide. *Courtesy of Sai Saha,* TV Guide Magazine.

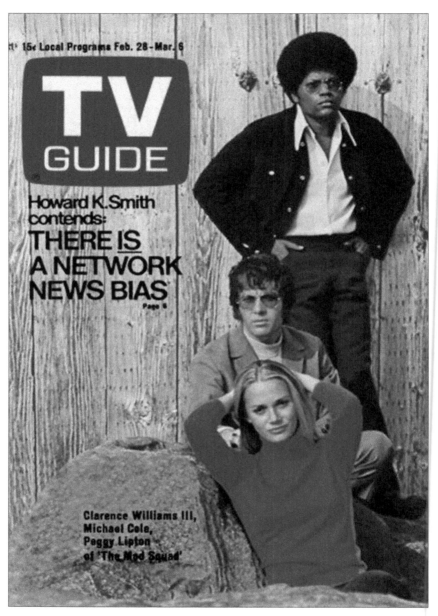

TV Guide. *Courtesy of Sai Saha*, TV Guide Magazine.

TV Guide. *Courtesy of Sai Saha,* TV Guide Magazine.

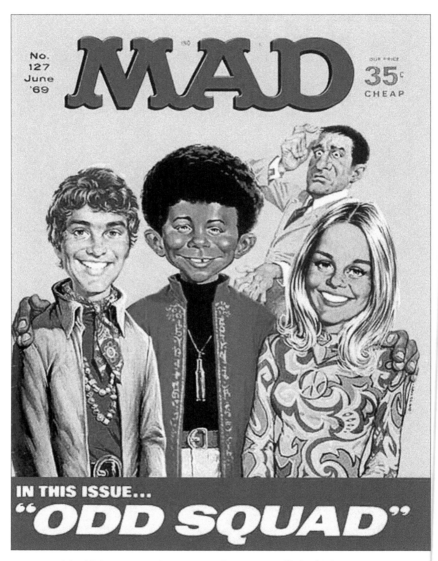

Mad Magazine, June 1969. Courtesy of Mad Magazine.

Jennifer Holly Cole, my Irish Colleen with sunset kissed hair.

Three of the four Logie Awards (Australia's Emmys) that I accepted on behalf of The Mod Squad, *which won for Best American Show 1971, 1972, 1973, 1974.*

My daughter, Jennifer, grown up and beautiful.

Beg, Borrow or Steal - *1973, Challenging part playing a disabled cop
with no hands. Courtesy of Universal Studios Licensing LLC.*

Me and Shelley.

Shelley and me on our wedding day, February 25, 1996.

The Mod Squad *reunited in 1997, at the SAG Awards, to present* ER *with the award for Best Ensemble Cast! Courtesy of NBCUniversal Media.*

Proud to have a role in Mr. Brooks, *starring Kevin Costner and Demi Moore - 2007. Courtesy of MGM Media Licensing.*

One of my favorite pictures of Shelley and me.

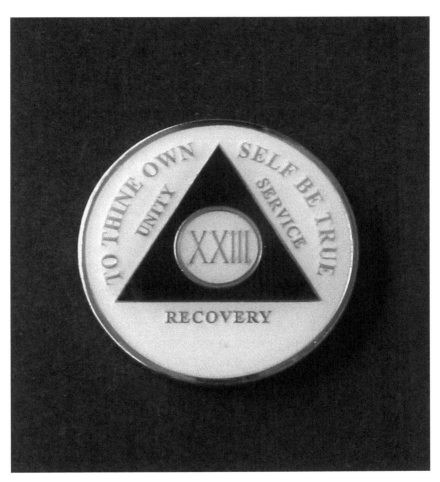

Grateful for 23 years of sobriety.

Chapter 8 – Fun & Games

I love sports and I love kids, so in 1969, when my friend and fellow actor, Dick Sargent (*Bewitched*), asked me if I wanted to go with him to UCLA and get involved with The Special Olympics, I agreed. I didn't know much about the organization, but I knew the Kennedys started it, and that was enough for me. Eunice Kennedy Shriver, JFK's sister, had seen that many children with handicaps and intellectual disabilities didn't even have a place to play, so she decided to take action. It started in her own backyard with the goal of seeing what sports these kids *could do,* not what they couldn't. Her vision grew into the Special Olympics movement. Anyway, I was so happy to be involved with this event and to rub elbows with great people like Eunice and Rafer Johnson, an Olympic gold medalist himself in the decathlon.

Watching these kids compete, kids in wheelchairs, leg braces, some blind, feeling their desire and will to succeed was overwhelming and powerful. I remember one girl about twelve years old who was a swimmer. I got word she wouldn't race until I came to watch her, so of course, I was there ASAP! She was so excited, and after big hugs, she was ready to go. The starter went off and away she went. She won! We both wept with joy when she received her gold medal.

Another athlete, a track runner, was in the 200-yard dash. About halfway there he fell and wouldn't get up. I ran out on the track with Jan Sarnoff (one of the board members). We helped him get up and once he was standing, the guy pulled away so hard and fast he almost broke my arm. He ended up passing everybody else and won the race! Again, lots of hugs and congratulations. If you ever get a chance, go and witness this amazing event. You'll never see these kids as "disabled" again.

After the incredible success of this first event, I was hanging out with Eunice, Jan, and Rafer and we came up with the idea for a "Winter Olympics" for these kids. When a Kennedy calls, you answer, so the next stop was Steamboat Springs, Colorado. I came up with a bright suggestion. How about I go downhill in a wheel-chair attached to a pair of skis (like one of the little cars I built out of orange crates as a kid)? I didn't think about the brakes, not that it would have done much good in all the snow. All the athletes and half the town came to watch this dumb shit. I ended up crashing into the hay bales and rolling over about ten times before wind-ing up on the skating pond! I wasn't hurt and I loved looking at all these kids cheering and laughing at the total ass I had made of myself. I should have won a medal for greatest fuckup.

Speaking of fuckups, every year during baseball season the Los Angeles Dodgers held a celebrity ball game. These are always great fun, and I was happy to be chosen to play first base by my celeb teammates. Please understand, I was never a great baseball player or fan—my sports were football (the Green Bay Packers) and bas-ketball (The LA Lakers). Anyway, the Celebrity team took the field first. I was nervous as hell when I heard the loudspeaker say, "And at first base . . . MICHAEL COLE!" I swear 50,000 people erupted in cheers. Now I was almost crying I was so nervous. Wouldn't you know the very first pitch was a ground ball coming fast as hell right at me? All I had to do was to stop the damn thing and touch first base. Well, the ball went right between my legs and out into right field. After that I heard the same crowd booing. I wanted to run away I was so embarrassed. Then Desi Arnaz Jr. saved my ass. The next pitch was a pop-up fly to Desi and he dropped it. All I could do was think, *thank you, Desi*. Needless to say, we lost about 1,000 to 3.

Now bowling was another thing. When I was about thirteen, I used to set pins at our hangout bowling alley. I was paid ten cents a lane. When we finished setting pins for the league bowlers, we would bowl until about two or three in the morning. There were five of us; we got to be really good. A couple of us had about a 180 average. We even formed a semi pro team . . . "The Bowl-a-Vard Wizkids." We would bowl at different alleys that sponsored their own teams, and we even won money. Back then setting pins was very physical work, and we worked two alleys at a time. Today it's all automated.

Fast forward to *The Mod Squad* years, and a very popular TV show called *Celebrity Bowling*. The winning celebrity team, if they bowled over 250, would win a new car for someone in the audience. Tige Andrews and I were asked to team up and compete. I knew Tige was pretty good; he was so strong he could almost throw the bowling ball overhand. And the two producers had a funny look on their faces when they saw me show up with two of my own bowling balls.

As I was walking in, I noticed a young girl, a *huge* fan, outside the studio. She was on her way to school, but I invited her to come in. I told her there was a chance to win a new car, so she eagerly joined us. I was determined to win that car for her. "Tige, the car is hers! Let's do this!"

I was up first. My first ball was a strike, a good pocket shot. I went again. My second ball was a strike. Not bad starting out with a double. Next Tige knocked down about eight pins and then picked up his spare. I had to go again. Strike! Three in a row; it's called a turkey. Tige spared again and on we went. The audience was going nuts, as was our young fan. Pretty soon the other celebs came out to watch. Sammy Davis Jr. was there and so was Ma since she was a very good bowler herself.

Tige and I rolled about a 265 game and we won that girl a brand-new car! They actually had to give the girl the keys to Tige's car on camera and then they went out to buy her one. Guess they never thought we would be that good!

I also had a blast doing the hugely successful game show, *Hollywood Squares*, which my friend Peter Marshall hosted. I was surrounded by incredibly funny people like George Gobel, Betty White, Charlie Weaver, and Paul Lynde. I sat in the square underneath Paul, and I swear I almost fell out of it with some of his answers. It was nonstop hilarity! I remember being relieved when I heard my question—"who was the first man to climb Mt. Everest"? I was happy I knew the answer—Sir Edmund Hillary!

There was another very popular program on ABC TV at that time called *The Dating Game*. I had never seen it, but when ABC asked if I would go on that show to promote *The Mod Squad*, I agreed. If you were a guest on the show, you sat behind a screen and had a list of silly questions to ask each of the three female contestants you couldn't see. They were vying to get you to pick them for your date. Based on their answers you chose one and then you would be sent on some elaborate trip. In this case, it was a trip to the famous Le Mans car race in France. That's the other reason I agreed to do the show.

Anyway, two of the girls were twins—beautiful blondes. I ended up picking one of them. The third girl was gorgeous too! Would have been fun to go with all three, but I never actually went on that date or that trip. I think there were conflicts with my shooting schedule. Thankfully, getting a date wasn't too tough for me; but my best date in those days was a Royal . . .

Crown Royal.

Chapter 9 – Paula

The Mod Squad continued to be a smash—and I continued getting smashed. Aaron started worrying about my being so wild. He thought if I got married it would tame me, straighten me out, and he kept encouraging me to "take the plunge." I was in no hurry. Paula and I had been together off and on during my first couple of years in Los Angeles. I went from sleeping in her backyard (and anywhere else I could find) to being on a hit TV show. Things were changing quickly.

During the hiatus of the second season of *The Mod Squad*, 1970, I had just gotten home from New York. Paula picked me up at LAX, and she was driving me to my house off Laurel Canyon. She had a big Lincoln Continental at the time. Laurel Canyon is a steep, winding canyon road, and water was always draining across it near the top. We had just started heading down when we crossed a wide, wet spot. She lost control of the car and it skidded and crashed head on into the side of the canyon wall, not once, but twice. I slammed into the windshield with my forehead and smashed my face open. Thank God, nothing happened to Paula's beautiful face. She suffered crack ribs, which is terribly painful.

I could feel the blood dripping all over. Even my boots were soaked with blood. People who lived nearby heard the impact and started coming out to help. (Of course there were no cell phones in those days.) One guy, who was a famous record producer, came running over with towels to try to stop the bleeding before two ambulances showed up—one for Paula and one for me.

I was losing a lot of blood, and the paramedics had to get me to the closest emergency room fast. There I was sewn up temporarily as best they could under the circumstances. Then I was taken to Mt. Sinai Hospital. It took hours of cleaning me up, picking pieces of glass from my scalp before the doctors could see the extent of the wounds and begin to go to work on me. It took over 300 stitches from my temple to my eyelid, which was stuck to the side of my nose, to the top of my skull to put me back together. Somehow I never lost consciousness, and I can tell you, it's weird to see your eye socket, your eyeball, and your skull exposed wide open like that. I could have played *The Phantom of the Opera* without the makeup or the mask!

I was then moved to a hospital room, more like a luxury suite in a hotel, which Aaron had arranged. He had been called from the first emergency stop, and raced to the hospital with his wife, Candy. I remember Aaron reaching under the blanket and taking my hand. He simply said, "I love you, Mick."

With round-the-clock nursing, meds, and a fully stocked bar, I was able to stay loaded and in no pain. I remember on the very first night someone holding the phone to my ear so I could hear the person who had called. It was Sammy Davis Jr. saying, "Man, thank God you didn't lose your eye like I did. I'll say a prayer and talk to you soon."

Clarence, Peg, and Tige called almost every day. Of course, Ma and my half-sisters, Deborah and Colleen, did too. I had moved them to Los Angeles after Lorell died - happy to have them near me.

I had a monitor so I could see who was coming down the hall-way. That was cool, since on occasion, a friend would sneak in some loaded brownies! We got stoned, even Ma, and I'll never forget how she laughed her ass off. There were notes, cards, flowers from fellow actors, fans, and friends; people were so kind and wonderful. That incredible energy helped me heal. Of course, I talked to Paula every day to make sure she was doing fine.

I was in the hospital for almost a month. That's a long time. I found myself thinking about a lot of things; a lot about my stepfa-ther. Why do I wear Lorell's ring? It was a huge question. We even did an episode about it. This was the guy who at one time threat-ened to shoot me with a .45 caliber! Still, I wanted him to see me wearing that ring on TV. It was important to me. Sadly, he never did. He died before the first *Mod Squad* episode aired. I had called him just before the show went on, and I knew he wasn't doing well at all. We talked for a few minutes and that was the last time I heard his voice. A piece of hope for a "father" went with him. Later, the ring was stolen when I was doing a play at some little theater, damn it. Somewhere along the line, I had started to feel Lorell as my dad. I think the reason was because at long last, I was truly making it on my own, my own way, and doing what came from within me.

The sense of a "father" bled over to Aaron. At a time when I could have died, he was the one by my side, caring for and about me. Our relationship was like a father/brother thing. I know I hurt Aaron. I let him down because of the booze. And I know we would have worked together again. I will always carry that guilt with me, but now I own it. It was my doing—no one else's. What I'm doing here is trying to be honest to both these father figures and myself, the alcoholic. I was happy and proud that years later, at least Aaron saw me sober.

We were able to start shooting season three of *The Mod Squad* on schedule, thanks to the talent of the lighting and makeup people, who did wonders to camouflage my scars, and to my Ray Ban sunglasses. All was damn near back to normal. That said, to this day, when I rub my eyelid I feel it tingle on the top of my head. Here I am once again, after all that shit, kept safe by my buddy Christ.

Toward the end of *The Mod Squad*, Paula and I made it official. I loved Paula; she was a good person, and it just seemed like the timing was right. The truth was, I didn't give much thought to the seriousness of marriage. It was more like, "why not"?

We were married in 1971. Paula was a beautiful bride. The ceremony was held at a church overlooking the ocean, followed by a big, splashy reception at the famous Chasen's in Beverly Hills—the "chic" restaurant to the stars. There were so many celebrities and show biz people there Aaron said I could write off the whole thing as a publicity event. It was a great party, and I was a champ at partying.

We honeymooned in Acapulco, and stayed at this fancy resort that was carved into the mountains with amazing views overlooking the ocean. We had a gorgeous suite, our own private swimming pool, and a well-stocked bar. Richard Burton and Elizabeth Taylor were rumored to be staying there too. We never saw them. I imagine if I had seen one of my idols, I would have fainted.

You would think nothing could go wrong in paradise, but it did. First off, it rained constantly and I mean poured. The ENTIRE time! The room flooded, I mean really flooded, not to mention the toilet. There was a huge boulder situated above our room that was threatening to give way at any moment. The final straw was the night before we were leaving, when we went to the five-star restaurant at the hotel. As we were walking in, Paula spotted another woman wearing the exact same expensive designer dress she had on. Paula went ballistic, crying hysterically. I tried to smooth things over by making light of it, but that only made it worse. Needless to say, the trip was pretty much a disaster. Not the most romantic way to spend a honeymoon, that's for sure.

From the beginning, it was pretty obvious that I was not the model husband. I mean, the whole reason I got married was because of pressure from others to "settle down" and that's obviously not the best reason to go into a marriage. But the amazing product of that union was our daughter, Jennifer, who was born in 1973. At long last I had the three things I always wanted: an Irish setter, a convertible sports car, and a beautiful little Irish "Colleen." From the moment I saw her, I fell in love with her soft complexion and beautiful "sunset hair." I loved our one-on-one time together when Paula resumed touring with The Modernaires. I changed diapers, fed her, walked her, took her to doctor checkups, and we played, endlessly. Sadly, that alone couldn't save our marriage.

Paula had two things to contend with—fame, and my ever-present drinking. Getting married didn't stop it, in fact it probably accelerated it because of the frustration we both felt. Too often I would stumble home late, smashed. Paula was increasingly insecure and jealous. We had screaming fights and ugly words were said that we both regretted later. This scene played out time and time again. Paula was hurt and I don't blame her. She tried to get me to stop drinking, but I was way too set in my ways.

To make things worse, when we first met, Paula was the one in the spotlight and now it was me. Being in a relationship with another performer is not easy, and my star was shining ever more brightly. I was on a hit television show and I was the one getting all the attention, doing interviews, being sought after, being recognized, my picture showing up in all the magazines. It was a total change from the way things had been and understandably, it became increasingly more difficult for her to handle.

We tried to maintain for Jennifer, living under the same roof but in separate parts of our house. Inevitably it just didn't work, and our marriage ended.

After the divorce, I was despondent. I needed time to think, to make sense of it all. That's when I packed up a few belongings and moved to a cabin in the woods of the Mullholland mountains. It really was a log cabin, built in 1928. Not much in the way of furnishings . . . a big arm chair, a TV, and an old redwood picnic table inside. It was quiet. Deer would stand out back and wait for a treat. It was me and my two cats, Cammie and Black, and booze. I needed to focus on the one thing that was crucial to my spirit—acting.

Chapter 10 - Australia

Mod Squad was a huge hit in Australia, but I had no idea just how big it was until I got a phone call telling me I had won some award for acting called the "Logie Award," like our Emmys. It really is a big deal down there and I was very surprised and honored! It took about twelve hours to fly to Sydney, with a refueling in Hawaii. But who cares! People from the blue-collar east side of Madison, Wisconsin, seldom got a chance to fly to Australia, let alone all expenses paid! Once I was settled in at the hotel, Jerry Feather-stone, the head of *TV Week* (their *TV Guide*), met me and we started walking to the theater, which was about four blocks away. As we approached, I could hear this absolute Beatlemania-like screaming. My new buddy said, "You hear that, Michael? That's for you! They know you're on your way. All the news channels have picked it up!" We rounded the corner and I couldn't believe it—there were thousands of screaming fans. We couldn't even get through the crowd until some of the cops and bodyguards jumped in and rushed me through a side door.

As I was escorted to the assigned table, I looked around and saw the audience was on its feet, applauding . . . for me! I was over-whelmed. You know, they say Australia is the land down under because it's below the equator. I told the people, I think the world is upside-down because Australia is really on top, at least in my book. I didn't know it at the time, but they have a saying when you really like someone, you call them "ON TOP!" That's the way I deeply felt about the Aussies. I loved how passionate and genuine they were. I also liked that they were drinkers, so naturally I fit right in.

When it finally came time for me to receive the Logie Award and my name was called, the place erupted. *The Mod Squad* won for Best American Television Show. I accepted the award and I of course thanked *TV Week* and all the people on behalf of our entire cast. Then I decided to recite *The Irish Prayer*. "Until we meet again, may God hold you in the palm of his hand." It was an amazing experience and I couldn't have asked for better treatment. Later, I celebrated with some of the local people and had a great time.

The next day, I had arranged to visit a children's hospital across the Sydney Bay. This was something I always tried to do when I was on the road. The beautiful little town of Manley sits right on the ocean. It reminded me of Carmel, California. The hospital is called The Royal Far West Children's Health Scheme. All services, the doctors and medical staff, food, beds, etc. are donated. It's similar to St. Jude's in the U.S. All the children there were from the outback, mostly from disadvantaged families. Most had never seen a body of water, let alone the ocean. I was given a tour of the facilities and was very impressed with the warmth and caring nature of the staff.

Then I joined the kids, many of whom were outside playing baseball. I noticed one young boy who was very kind, helping the other kids with handicaps to fit in the game. His name was Stephen. I was so impressed with him I wanted to be sure he could afford to stay for as long as he needed. I was able to do that by "sponsoring a bed" for him until he was well.

One of my favorite moments was with a little Aboriginal girl, about six or seven years old. She had a little 45 rpm record player and was sitting listening to music. I came over, picked her up, and we danced to some great rock and roll songs. She held me around the neck so tight I couldn't help but feel the love from this precious child. The fact that she had been born without any legs meant nothing; she had an amazing spirit and zest for life. I held on to her and we danced for what seemed like hours. She went right to my heart and she is still there.

The entire Australian experience was one I could never forget, so I was ecstatic when a couple of years later in 1973, I was invited back to the Logie Awards, this time being held in Melbourne. In addition to *The Mod Squad* winning Best American Show again, I was there because the people asked me to come back. They had a special Logie Award to present me. The fans were wonderful; even the weather was perfect. However, I had a way of fucking up nice situations.

I was seated at a table with the great actor Glenn Ford, also a great guy and a great drinker. I had already been up on the stage once to accept the award for Best American Show. I was very proud and grateful to represent our cast. I sat back down thinking I was done. So it was time to get the party started! It didn't take me long to down a few whiskeys. Believe me, the shit they drink down there does not fool around. Sure enough, as I was well into inebriation, they called me back up on stage to present me with a Token of Friendship award. I was totally shocked. I made it up there ok and managed a slurry "thank you from the bottom of my heart." As the applause grew, I choked up, and tears welled up. Embarrassed I said, "Oh shit!"

Well, the Rupert Murdoch people were running the show, and since I had uttered the first word of profanity to be broadcast on Australian TV, they shut the rest of the show completely down! Talk about a disaster!

Two things really saved my ass.

One, as I was leaving the theatre the people outside were yelling, "You were great, mate! We love you, Michael!" They didn't care.

The other took place the next day. I had made plans to return to the same children's hospital I had visited on my previous trip. Unbeknownst to me, they had arranged a huge welcome back party. It was wonderful. The staff and kids had made a huge cake for me.

How's this? One day the headlines were "Michael Cole Swearing on TV," and the next day the headlines were, "Children at Royal Far West Welcome Back Michael Cole with Love." I later learned that my swearing on TV had garnered more attention for *The Logie Award Show* than it had ever had. I'm not proud of my behavior, but I will say the entire experience created a bond between me and the Aussies that has lasted to this day.

Chapter 11 — Giving Back

While I missed the challenges of being on a hit series when *The Mod Squad* ended, I realized that I had new opportunities. I could act in plays, I could guest star on other TV shows, and I could do something that was becoming increasingly important to me—work with charities close to my heart, especially those involving children: The Braille Institute, Special Olympics, and children's hospitals. It was a way for me to use this strange thing called fame to help others. I wanted to make a difference in children's lives so they would have things a little better than I did.

I got to be real close friends with the stunt guys from the show. We had the best stuntmen in the world, part of the organization called Stunts Unlimited. Ronnie Rondell, who was as good as it gets, was my stunt double. We were the same age, and he looked so much like me that he could stand outside my trailer and sign autographs for me as a joke. One day I said to Ronnie, "let's get a bunch of the guys and go over to the Braille Institute". The idea was that even those these kids couldn't see, we could give them the experience of riding a motorcycle. They could hear and feel the sounds, vibrations the engines roar up close.

The kids were so excited, it was beautiful. I'd get on a bike with one of the kids, and say, "OK, now I'm gonna hold the clutch in. Now you put your hand on mine. OK, you feel that?" Now the bike is running. I'd put my foot on his and click it in to gear. I'd start to let the clutch out a little bit, and you can really start to feel the power in the thing! It came together beautifully. From then on, every time they heard a motorcycle on TV they knew what the hell it was. They'd actuality ridden one! You could see the excitement in their opaque eyes.

We also brought a "trick" horse that was trained to fall down when it heard a gun shot. I said to the kids, "We'll do a run by, and you guys stand right here as close as possible to the horse, and you'll hear him, the hooves coming around the track." And the kids are going, "Whoa!" Their eyes getting as big as saucers. I said, "Ok, now what we're gonna do is fire a gun." We rigged it up to where the horse fell, oh, maybe ten feet from the kids so they could hear all that. The horse went down and the kids just went crazy! They could feel the dirt fly up from the ground as the horse fell. The horse stayed down. I went over and checked. I said, "She's fine, she's lying down."

Then I said, "Kids, come here. Pet the horse and thank her because she's got a little secret that she wants to tell you—she's blind in one eye. So next time you've got to do something that's hard because you're blind, just think of this horse, and she'll help you do it." It opened up so much of a world for them. Nothing in a movie would ever be the same for them again. That really put a whole new dimension into their lives. They'll hear a horse in a Western, or they'll hear a motorcycle chase, and they'll be right there in the moment.

I think it was during the first holiday season after the show ended that I got a call from the University of Wisconsin Hospital. There was a young girl, around ten or eleven, who was very ill with cancer and had been asking for me. When I heard that, I made up my mind and immediately flew to Madison. It was Christmas Eve. The University Hospital is a research facility, mostly for the terminally ill. I remember as I was walking up the front steps, there was a light snow falling—just enough to hear the snow crunching beneath my feet. It reminded me of walking to church on Christmas Eve many years earlier.

I admit I was anxious because I didn't know what to expect. I entered the large, empty lobby, my footsteps echoing, not a soul around. It was late. As I made my way down a long hallway, a hospital representative finally approached me. She immediately recognized me, and knew why I was there. As she led me to the girl's room, she told me how very excited she was to see me, as I was to see her.

The young people who I have met in hospitals such as St. Jude's always make me feel at ease with their acceptance of their lives, and their conditions. To me there is nothing more contradictory to innocence than a sick or frightened child. I believe these young people are next to God, and like most seriously ill children I have met, they haven't one ounce of self-pity. She was no different.

Her room was covered with pictures of me and the show. Despite how obviously weak and sick she was, she immediately brightened up when I came in. I gave her a gentle hug, pulled up a chair, and we talked for several hours about my adventures on *The Mod Squad*, and also about her hopes and dreams. I could see she was tiring and it was time to go. I kissed her good-bye. As I was leaving her room I was taken by surprise, because I saw an elderly couple, very traditional, rural Wisconsin-looking people, standing in the dark corner of the room. They were in shadow, illuminated only by outside Christmas lights blinking through the window.

They told me they were her grandparents, and they had been there the entire time. They didn't know *The Mod Squad*, or who I was, but with tears in their eyes, they told me how much my visit meant to them and more importantly to their granddaughter. I held them both for a minute, and then I left. By the time I got to my hotel there was a message. Like the pure white snow that had fallen earlier, the young girl was gone. She was among the angels.

My cousin, who lives in Madison, told me a few years later that a nurse friend of hers relayed an amazing story to her. There was a little boy who was very sick in that same hospital, and in his delirium, spoke of being visited by a young girl who comforted him, saying, "Don't worry, everything is going to be all right. Michael is here." However, there was no young girl in the hospital at the time.

I'm no angel, that's for sure, but according to at least one fan, I am a guardian angel. In 2009, I received an envelope postmarked from France. The letter I found inside so moved me that I want to share it. I'll let my dear friend Catherine tell it in her own words, with her broken English, because I find it so touching and poignant. Imagine her beautiful, soft spoken voice as you read it:

1971. I'm 15 years old. I live in Dinard, a well-known seaside town in Bretagne, very close from the Normandy beaches landings and not far from the Mont St Michel, one of the most beautiful spots in France. It's a mystic place, an island off the coast with a cathedral rising up out of it, a medieval fairy tale palace. My grandparents were owners of a little pub called Freddy's Bar; most of their customers were English and American people. They used to come there to drink their famous Irish coffee. There I spend a happy youth between them and my parents. In this place I learn to speak English very young.

My Grand Pa receive many English TV channels, and one day I was at his apartment, and by chance I discover The Mod Squad. *First of all I hear that very special sound of the theme music. It's like a magnet to me. I look at the screen and see the name of this episode is "You can't tell the players without a program." Michael's voice, it was his way of acting, with true feelings and with love. He wasn't just playing a character, Pete Cochran and he were the same person. I think that's the reason why* The Mod Squad *was such a success.*

In this episode a young lady is attempting to suicide herself. She has nobody to talk to about her problems, and Michael tells her, "Try me!" He wants to help her, to care for her, and he tells her, "Sooner or later you're gonna have to have faith." Those words! I needed to hear them, it was Michael on screen talking to me through the screen and from that I feel strength.

I was in so bad shape. Some days before, tragic event touched me very deeply. I lost a very close friend from an accident. That was catastrophic event for me. I was living in a loving family. There's no problem there at all. It is easy to speak to your loving parents or adoring grandparents, but sometimes you need to have somebody your own age to talk about many things, to be your confidante.

I said, "My God, I have to have faith, and I have to go home. I am happy, have loving parents, grandparents and friends, so go home and carry on with your life." And from that moment on I really considered Michael my guardian angel.

I want to end with that sadness!! I hear your voice at that moment, you're acting with such conviction, and it sounds so true that I take those words personally. You're talking to me, making me realize that my whole life is before me. I feel a new strength in myself at that moment. You have become my "guardian angel."

This day I made a promise to myself: one day, I have to make you know that story! And I keep that thought in the deep of my heart. I'm sure that The Mod Squad *helped other people to make good decisions, or prevent them from doing bad things.*

Now, it's 2009. I'm 53 years old. During the past 38 years I keep a little picture of you in my purse (that I found in a French TV magazine) and put it in a little gold medallion I have of Jesus and two angels. The one I send to you Michael. So now it's time for me to dare to find a way to contact you, but how? I'm so far away and you are unreachable. I finally tell the story to a very close friend named Dany C, she gives me the phone number of a friend of hers living in Florida. She's sure he could help me. I call him, he doesn't know me at all, but he wants to help. Eight days later he gives me a phone number. There again is God with me. I called. Probably surprised by a call from France, they give me an address to send you a letter.

I write this letter and send it. I'm so happy I succeed. You are now going to know what you have done for me this day of 1971; 38 years later it's just amazing. We have an expression. We say that "faith can make the mountains move," but for me you know but for me the faith has made the ocean disappear between me and you.

The first call comes telling me you want to talk with me. I can't believe it!!! Finally, after all those years, on the 10th of November 2009, I'm talking with my guardian angel.

To think that you were able to reach out over a thousand miles of ocean and save another human being's life. Give them hope. It's a profound example of the power of television, and the responsibility. Because of *The Mod Squad*, I was given the opportunity to come into people's lives in odd ways, and unlikely places, and sometimes, to make a difference. I was blessed with this gift, and giving back when I can is the way I have to honor it.

Chapter 12 - After the Squad

The Mod Squad was a great ride, for five seasons—over one hundred episodes. It worked so well because the cast, the crew, everyone liked coming to work each day, most of the time. I was glad to be working steadily with people I loved. In fact, I even went to Aaron on my own during the fifth season and told him I'd be willing to come back for as long as he needed me. I didn't feel like the writing or quality had changed, like was often the case with shows after so long. I believed if you're taking the money, you have to find a way to earn it, so I never walked through a scene—ever. I took it seriously. The show was still very popular so that wasn't the problem.

But eventually things started to unravel.

Clarence was ready to get back to the stage. Peg was in love with Quincy Jones and was ready to start a family. Our contracts were up and they might have re-upped us, but the network was happy with five seasons, and I could tell things were changing. It was a good time to stop. I could feel Aaron was starting to pull away, focusing more on new projects he had in development.

Also the other networks had finally started to gain some leverage with the big shows they kept scheduling against us. They were serious about lowering our ratings, and their determination was obvious.

For me, it was mixed emotions the last year. My first thought was about losing the money and security but that was soon surpassed by how much I'd miss our family on the show. It was like saying goodbye to your loved ones forever. We were such a close-knit cast and crew, and we had a handful of great directors who loved the show and were with it the entire time.

Earl Bellamy was one. He did a lot of television. They called him "Old Blue." Earl was a champion guy who everybody loved. He was one of the few directors who kept us on time. He did his home-work. He never said "action," just "go!" And he didn't say, "cut." We would wait for him to say, "This one's for the pinto mouse." That meant it was the last shot. We never understood where that expression came from, but we loved it and we loved him.

Aaron offered me the chance to direct an episode the final season—I knew my way around the camera, but I knew I couldn't focus on that. Besides, I wasn't interested in the editing and re-shooting that came with it. I just like what happened in the moment.

As I write this, I find I remember so many of those moments like they were yesterday. It all comes back to me. Recently I watched the pilot on DVD and was surprised how well it still worked. I kept saying "damn this is good!" The music knocked me out. The writing was so good. Each of us had a moment together—me with Clarence, me and Peg, Peg and Clarence, talking from the heart about how we got where we were. Tige was the cement that held us all together. It's so hard to believe that those five years were fifty years ago!

After *The Mod Squad* was off the air, there was a letdown. I didn't miss the day-to-day, but I missed the people. The lonelier I got, the more I drank. I was burnt out and I didn't really care. I was offered three different series—one with a popular producer named Quinn Martin. Aaron had another one too, but I wanted a break from that routine. I wanted to do a movie or maybe some theater. I wanted to do the only thing that ever came naturally to me. I wanted to act.

Chapter 13 – Acting Out

In 1971 I starred in a movie of the week that Aaron produced called, "The Last Child," with Academy Award winner Van Heflin, Ed Asner, Harry Guardino, and Janet Margolin—one hell of a cast. It was a futuristic story taking place in a badly overpopulated country, where each couple was only allowed one child and people over sixty-five were forbidden medical care under a very draconian set of laws. It was a really good film, and earned a Golden Globe nomination!

Following that, I did another film for television called "Beg, Borrow or Steal" with Mike Connors, and Kent McCord—terrific guys. We were three ex-cops, disabled while on duty. My character had no hands. I did the entire movie using "hooks" for hands. We had a guy on set who worked with me and taught me how to use them. I even had a scene where I had to thread a needle with those hooks. The movie was ok, but the role was physically challenging.

Then I was offered the part of Brick in *Cat on a Hot Tin Roof* in New Orleans. I jumped at the chance to do legitimate theater and have a role that would give me the opportunity to pull out all the stops . . . to dig into the character and do my best work. For example, I called the local zoo to find out about a beautiful Bengal tiger that was there. I asked if I could come over at feeding time and watch the tiger. They slid a big chunk of meat through the cage door and left it open for her. They placed the meat next to a bowling ball. I watched as this beautiful beast lowered her body close to the ground and stealthily stalked the meat, growling, ears back, baring her lethal, beautiful teeth. She's thinking the bowling ball is going to get her meat, so with one stunningly fast whack, that sixteen-pound ball was tossed aside like a ping pong ball. Then she grabbed the meat and made her way back through the door. In my mind, that tiger became Maggie in the play. That image is what I used as an actor as I wrestled with Maggie's betrayal—her having had sex with my buddy, who was now dead. She would do *anything* to get to Brick.

In the opening scene, Brick comes from the shower on crutches, a cast on his broken leg. His first line is, "Shut up, Maggie. You want me to hit you with this crutch, Maggie? I will hit you with the crutch, Maggie." The anger and raw emotion was real, as I saw in Maggie that tiger, and my buddy as the piece of meat. The actress playing Maggie got scared every night. Of course, I never hit her, but I wanted to. That was Maggie the Cat that whacked that ball at the zoo!

I never drank during these performances, but afterward they had a big glass of Crown Royal waiting for me in the dressing room. I was emotionally spent. I'd sit listening to gospel music and sip on that and think about how I would have killed Maggie because she fucked my best friend.

One night after the show I was sitting in my dressing room calming down, getting ready for the next night, when there was a knock on my door. A former lover of Tennessee Williams (who wrote the play) had come to see the show several times. This night he came backstage to offer his congratulations. He said, "That is exactly the way Tennessee would have wanted Brick to be played." What a compliment that was, coming from this man who loved Tennessee so much. I toured with *Cat* for about a year, and as grueling as it was, it was an incredible experience.

After the run of the play, some people from the Eye Research Centre in New Orleans asked me if I would be willing to help them raise a few dollars for a little girl, about six. She was a beautiful little thing who was going blind and needed to have an operation to restore her sight. Of course I would do anything I could to help. They held a telethon where I made an appearance and I spent the evening answering phones. Several months later, after she had her operation, there was a ceremony being filmed to celebrate her recovery. Her mom and dad were there at the studio on the side of the stage. There was a big camera cable on the floor. She comes walking toward me and all of a sudden she stopped and looked down, saw the cable, and stepped over it. That was a beautiful moment. I knew she saw that cable! It's moments like that that make you realize that sometimes being a celebrity allows you to be part of the real stuff of life.

The next play I did was *Wait until Dark* with Deana Martin. We opened in a little town outside Chicago called Sullivan, Illinois, to get the bugs out before going into Chicago. From there, we toured for about six months. Deana is the daughter of Dean Martin, and a wonderful singer and actress. We had met a few years earlier through Peggy, who introduced us at the wrap party for the pilot of *The Mod Squad*. We hit it off right away and started hanging out. I really liked her dad, who was very nice to me. I remember he would come home after a day on the golf course. Cadillac had even built him a special station wagon to hold his golf clubs. What impressed me was that he always tried to make it home to have dinner with his family every night.

Deana was an amazing partner to work with in *Wait until Dark*. She played the blind protagonist (Audrey Hepburn in the movie) and I was the evil bad guy, of course. During one of the performances in the last act, "Susy" turns out all the lights so that my character, who is trying to kill her, can't see either. Now we are on equal footing. She hears me moving around in the dark and stabs me in the back with a butcher knife. I manage to get up, exit off stage, where I get a can of gasoline intending to douse the apartment and set it on fire. Just before I reenter, I accidentally slipped on some spilled gas (water), hit my head on an iron safe, which was part of the set, and fell off the stage. I felt my real blood streaming down my face. But, the show must go on. I literally couldn't see a thing, so I crawled over and whispered to a guy sitting in the first row, asking him to help me get back on stage to make my entrance. He did.

This final scene is scary. I lunge at Susy with my knife, "Geraldine." The audience gasped as I leapt out from stage right, my face covered in blood. Deana *really* screamed when she saw the blood covering my face. Susy had forgotten the one light that didn't turn off—the light to the fridge. I drag myself across the floor, open the fridge door, and wedge a towel in so she can't shut it. Just at that moment, when I am on the verge of killing her, I collapse and die. Susy runs to the front door and her husband is there. She's safe. Curtain! I wound up with about ten stitches but I didn't care. Actually, I liked it! Method acting!

By the time the run was over, I wanted to be home. I missed Jennifer and wanted to have time with her. It was time to get back to television.

I started doing a number of guest appearances. *Police Story* was fun because I worked with Don Meredith. We had a great time! I did an episode of *Wonder Woman* because Jennifer, who was about seven at the time, loved that show. Lynda Carter was very nice. I thought she was very gutsy to wear her costume. I didn't know anything about the concept of the show when we started filming. In one scene Wonder Woman had just landed her "invisible" airplane. *What? It's invisible?* I had no clue what was going on, but it was fun.

I also did guest shots on some of Aaron's new shows—*Vegas, Fantasy Island.* One of my favorites to this day is a scene I did for *The Love Boat.* That show was kind of "light-hearted," about finding love and adventure, but this particular episode had a more intense story line. My character was in a wheelchair because I had gotten shot while serving in the Vietnam War. I was paralyzed from the waist down. The other guest star was John Rubinstein. In the story, we had been best friends in high school, but he had gone to Canada to avoid the draft and I ended up wounded in the war. There was a class reunion held on the ship, and Johnny's character was ashamed to see me. He felt tremendous guilt for the good life he had, compared to mine. We had an emotional confrontation—just the two of us, in a dark, cavernous ballroom onboard. It was powerful, and I was proud of the work. When the crew applauds after a scene, you've done something right. Many of them were in tears.

These occasional TV jobs were fun, but they weren't enough to satisfy me creatively. I was at a crossroads trying to figure out what to do next. You go through changes. Art that I never understood started to make sense to me. I started to think more deeply about the creative process—about everything. And I was drinking heavily. Without the TV series, I didn't have the same people looking out for me. I was on my own. I had lost my focus. I didn't have a relationship, I was lonely, and by then I was gaining a reputation due to my drinking. That meant offers were sputtering.

I secluded myself in the mountain cabin, coming in to town only to meet someone for a drink. Being alone with my thoughts meant I was alone with copious amounts of alcohol. Thoughts of guilt led to self-destructive behavior as I started reassessing so many things: the failed marriages, the fights, friends I had lost along the way. It wasn't really about wanting to kill myself, it was worse. My creativity had always been my salvation—my identity. I had lost it to booze. I was so drunk I didn't know what direction I was going in and I didn't care. Eventually I found myself in the same place as I was in Madison, all those years ago—alone and depressed.

Then in 1978, Ma, the center of my world, died. As E.E. Cummings once wrote, "If there are any heavens, my mother will (all by herself) have one." Ma's death was the final straw. My heart was broken, and my spirit. Everything was falling apart. I stayed in the cabin, isolated and depressed and drunk. Years passed with only the occasional TV role, but with my bad reputation growing, it was only a matter of time before the phone stopped ringing completely. There were a couple of short-lived female relationships, but really the only thing that was constant was my drinking. I was truly dying of alcohol.

Chapter 14 - Shelley

By 1989, everything in my life had fallen apart. My beloved mother had died, my marriage was long gone, and my career was practically nonexistent. An actor's life is filled with highs and lows, and I knew that going into it. My glory days on *The Mod Squad* were now fading into celluloid history and in this business, you have to stay in the public eye to maintain any kind of career momentum. My reputation as a bankable actor had eroded. The decades of alcohol abuse were taking their toll on me physically and emotionally.

On July 7, 1989, some friends who were frankly worried about me asked me to come down from the woods and join them to listen to a wonderful jazz singer at a club we went to occasionally. As we walked into Monteleone's I spotted another old friend, Karen, at the bar and I paused to say hello. She introduced me to *her* friend—a beautiful woman named Shelley. We instantly struck up a conversation, and I found myself incredibly drawn to her . . . her looks, her style, she was funny, articulate . . . there was something different about her; I felt it from the start. Believe it or not, in those first moments, a voice whispered to me, in my heart, "It's her, Michael." I silently responded, "I know, Ma. I know." (I still wish they could have met each other.)

Shelley and I talked until closing, and I didn't want the evening to end. I asked if she would come back to my cabin and she agreed. She followed me up the dark, winding roads leading up the mountain trusting her instincts, she later told me, that I was a gentleman. We talked and laughed for hours. I was trying not to drink too fast because I didn't want to screw this up. Just like when I had an acting job, I'd never drink at work, but after they said "cut" it was a different story. So I was pacing my drinks, and actually pacing back and forth as we talked. I think for the first time in my life, I was nervous around a woman . . . but in a good way. I put on one of my favorite Bob Dylan albums. I truly was *Knocking on Heaven's Door.*

We talked about everything from poetry to philosopher Albert Camus to the LA Lakers. I wanted to soak in the evening and make this feeling last. I fell in love that night.

Around four AM (not an unusual hour for me), I could see she was getting tired. My heart skipped a beat when she said she had to go. She was sitting at the picnic table in the middle of the room. I remember I walked over to the bench, gently lifted her up by her shoulders and kissed her. I never wanted someone so much so fast in my life. Without another word, we headed outside and got into our cars. I led her back down the curvy, dark road to the bottom of the mountain, and we both pulled over. I went over to her car window, leaned in, and kissed her for a second time.

"Can I see you tomorrow?" I asked.

"It's already tomorrow," she replied with a smile.

"Well, I'll call you later."

I kissed her once more and watched her drive away until I could barely make out the taillights. The minute I got home, I called and left a message. I wasn't going to let her forget me. Besides, I did want to be certain she made it home safely. (She told me later those "manners" made a huge impression.)

That next day we met late in the afternoon at the Sportsmen's Lodge, a landmark restaurant and hotel with beautiful grounds, a lake with swans, and a bench not too different from the one at my cabin. We talked, we walked, we held hands, and we kissed and talked and kissed. The desire was palpable. Later we were making out in my car like frustrated teenagers. I couldn't get enough of her.

Days following that she would go to work, I would call, we would arrange to meet somewhere for cocktails. I got excited every time I walked into a place and she was there. I loved holding her in my arms. I was still a fixture on the bar scene and there wasn't a bar or restaurant where people didn't know me and were so happy to see me walk in with this woman on my arm. The bartender would pour us drinks, and we would launch into conversation. I loved hearing about her day, her work, and her career. Plus, Shelley just fit in anywhere. She could laugh and joke with the "guys" and yet was always a class act.

I was used to dating women in the entertainment industry for the most part, so this beautiful, self-sufficient woman with a high-powered career was a totally different experience. Shelley was the Los Angeles director of *GQ Magazine* when we met. I found out she had married young and was divorced following a ten-year relationship. She struggled financially until she found her niche working in advertising sales for major name publications: *Rolling Stone* magazine, *George* (the one started by John F. Kennedy, Jr.), and then *GQ*, the men's style magazine, when we met. She had been single for many years, tired of the dating scene, and was content to focus on her career. It was a refreshing change to meet a successful, stable, independent woman who was also beautiful. She was self-assured and secure. I really respected her.

We saw each other every single day from the day we first met. As the weeks went by, I shared more of my stories from *The Mod Squad* and life in the world of acting. She has a degree in Theater from the University of Washington, so she understood my world. She was interested and intrigued, but having been around celebrities in her business she wasn't star-struck or obsessed. That too was a refreshing change from women I typically met.

How's this for irony? We discovered that our paths *were* to have crossed some twenty years earlier, but God or Destiny or the Universe interfered. Turns out Richard, Shelley's then-husband, was the Director of Advertising and Promotion for the ABC affiliate in Portland, Oregon. Clarence and I were on a press tour for the premier of *The Mod Squad* and we were scheduled to make an appearance there, after which we would have dinner with Richard and his wife. To no one's surprise, CW and I had gotten a little rowdy so they cut our junket short. They sent Tige in to replace us so that first meeting between Shelley and me never happened. I knew that this time I wasn't going to let her get away. That meant "downplaying" my drinking.

Given the life of an out-of-work actor, I'd drink all night, sleep half the day, maybe take a hike, clean up, and anxiously await the hour when Shelley got off work. We would meet for a drink, dinner, she would come to my house, but most frequently I'd go to her condo since she had to be up early the next day. I would tuck her in, kiss her goodnight, and then I could hit a bar or two on the way home and she'd never know. Win, win.

We enjoyed helping each other with our careers. She would get very excited when I had an audition. She liked running lines with me. In 1990, I won the role of Henry Bowers in the TV miniseries, *IT* (based on the Stephen King novel). Before I landed the job, I spent the week rehearsing for the audition at her place. One day she came home from work to find me stalking back in forth in her living room with a frightening, maniacal grin on my face and a kitchen knife in my hand. She understood.

IT was shot on location in Vancouver with an incredible cast: the extraordinary Tim Curry, Annette O'Toole, John Ritter, Richard Masur, and Harry Anderson. The story revolved around a sadistic clown called Pennywise who could transform himself into his prey's worst fears. I played the adult Henry Bowers, who as a kid had been so traumatized by IT that he went mad. His hair had turned white from the shock and terror of his encounter. I had spent years locked in an insane asylum until IT returned and helped me to escape to kill everyone who threatened him. The show was a huge ratings hit, with seventeen million people watching it. To this day, *IT* has a cult following . . . and I'm still afraid of clowns!

In 1991, I booked a recurring role in what was, unfortunately, a short-lived comedy series, *Good Sports*, starring Ryan O'Neal and Farrah Fawcett. I didn't know my ass from first base when it came to comedy, which is why, I was told, that I was funny! It was great working with my old friends and to be in front of the camera again.

Later that same year, I joined the cast of *General Hospital* as a series regular. I learned quickly that shooting a soap opera is a totally different thing than a regular series. It's a totally different approach. For example, the cameras only roll in the afternoon. The actors have ten to thirteen pages of dialogue daily. This is new material each day, and often the sides are delivered to your door the night before for scenes to be shot the next afternoon.

You spend the morning in makeup, camera rehearsal, and blocking—where to sit, to stand, to walk. Obviously the camera, crew, and the actors have to be on the same page, because there isn't time for do-overs. After a few days, I had a totally new respect for soap opera casts, crew, and even the casting people. I played the part of the evil Harlan Barrett, the head of a cartel. Once I got in the rhythm of the routine, I enjoyed it. One of the nicest things that happened was that I got to work with Jane Elliot. She is an excellent actress, and ironically, she was in one of the early episodes of *The Mod Squad!* I had the chance to work with Tony Geary, the star of GH for years! We became close friends both on and off the set.

All good things must come to an end, and after about six months, it was time to kill off my character. My final scene was with Tony after I had been shot. On every television show, there is an advisor from the network's Standards and Practices department who monitors it for anything deemed "inappropriate." So here I am, in this very dramatic death scene, dying in Tony's arms. We worked really hard to make this as believable as it could be. I chose to die with my *eyes open,* which is real. Tony then reached over and shut them. It was a touching scene. But, after reviewing it, word came down from "above" that I couldn't do that. It was *too* real. What the fuck? Why not? Tony and I were pissed. He had recently lost his father and was particularly emotional about this. He knew what I did was right. Anyway, we wound up shooting it their way just to move on and not battle the system, but we were both angry as hell!

Throughout this period, I was proud that my celebrity was beneficial to Shelley. She frequently asked me to join her for client dinners and other business-related social events. I enjoyed meeting her business associates and it felt like we were a team. I respected her enough to watch what I drank. She would prompt me to tell my Hollywood stories, and then I'd sit back and watch her in action. Damn she was good!

We had fun doing everything together. We went to the movies, the theater, and since we are both sports nuts, we would go to Lakers games and watch Magic Johnson do his thing. Shelley is also a Seahawks fan; I bleed green for the Green Bay Packers, so we seldom missed watching football on the weekends. It was neat sharing that too. It was an easy and comfortable "courtship."

When Shelley and I went out, it never failed that a woman would recognize me, approach me, and tell me how much they loved me/ Pete. I'd respond with a warm smile and a hug, but I made sure my other arm was around her. I would draw her in close to me at those moments to make sure she knew that she was the one—and always would be if she'd let it be. I'd had plenty of experience with women, but dating and relationships were just never a priority. I guess my track record proves that. You might be surprised that I was never a "player," despite what the fan magazines might have suggested. Even during the height of fame, during the hysteria, the guys on the set would say, somewhat jealously, "You can have as many women as you want, Michael. Why are you hanging out at a bar with friends?" The truth was that was where I was most comfortable. I always enjoyed the company of women, but the bottle was clearly my first love, and not nearly as complicated.

When Shelley and I became intimate, it was perfect and beautiful, coming together like I had never known. The first night was tender, gentle, exploring. We were two people who had been alone for a long time, and we were filled with longing, crashing together, incredibly passionate. We couldn't get enough of each other and spent hours together into the dawn. I wanted to hold her and never let her go. I don't know how she was able to keep to her work schedule, but somehow she managed. I would call her several times a day at the office, and I couldn't wait for her to get home. It has been like that ever since. All these years later it has never changed.

The next year seemed to go by quickly. We were happy, so in love, and I felt like I was keeping the drinking to a manageable level, at least in front of her. But I'm an alcoholic, and I could only maintain the veneer for so long. It was inevitable. I would get drunk and totally lose track of time, calling her at three or four in the morning. At first, she seemed to chalk it up to my actor's life. Later I think she started to realize *she* was in denial and didn't want to see the truth. It was too scary.

After *General Hospital,* the auditions were few and far between. My late nights out were increasing, and Shelley was growing more and more upset. It was a recipe for disaster. There were so many times where I thought she was going to confront me, give me an ultimatum. Each time I was able to pull myself together, apologize, charm her, and manage to have just a couple of drinks when we were together, knowing I'd hit some bar after I left her place. It was an exhausting roller-coaster ride; a double life is not what I had envisioned and I knew it was going to catch up to me. I just didn't know how to stop it. Eventually Shelley had no choice but to admit to herself that I was a full blown alcoholic. She tried to stop me, to control it, to hide the liquor. She begged me to get help and I made promises that I could never keep. Alcoholism is too devious and conniving.

By 1993, things were at the breaking point. We would talk, I'd deny that I had a problem, she would get angry, I'd try to slow down and it would seemingly get better, but that cycle repeated over and over. I hated myself for causing her so much pain. She cried, begged, cajoled, but never once did she threaten to leave me. I think at that time she knew that she couldn't. God knows I never wanted her to.

Something had to give, and it was Shelley who took the first step by starting to see a counselor to get help. She began to learn about co-dependency. I could sense a shift in her. She was talking more about making changes and not compromising. She was getting stronger emotionally and I was getting scared, which led to her finally persuading me to see a counselor as well.

She found a guy who was considered an expert in addiction/recovery. When I met Ray, in the spring of 1993, we clicked right away. I liked him because he was soft spoken, intelligent, easy to talk to, and had a deeply spiritual side that resonated with me. We talked about my goal to "control" the drinking, and that was what we agreed I would work on. Shelley was skeptical of this approach, but she gave me space. Then it happened.

The week before Christmas, we were invited to a holiday party being given at a jewelry store owned by a dear friend of Shelley's family. Steve is a warm, loving guy, who was always kind to me, and it sounded like it would be fun. The plan was to go after Shelley got home from work. I stopped at a bar to have "just one" before picking her up (yeah . . . right) because I knew I could only have one in front of her at the party. Well, one drink led to who knows how many, and when I walked in the door, late and drunk, I could see it on her face. She knew I was smashed and I knew she was done! I don't remember everything that was said, but I do remember storming out in anger because I couldn't take it. I ended up going to the jewelry store myself. I'm not sure why I did that or even how I got there, but it was a big mistake. Steve immediately called Shelley out of concern and told her that I was there and I was a mess. I had definitely hit my bottom.

Three days later, when I opened the door to Ray's office, I knew something was going on. Shelley and her therapist Mark were there. I sat down on the couch next to Shelley and took her hand in mine. God I loved her.

Ray stood up and said quietly, "Michael, I'm sorry, but in all good conscience, I can't continue to see you and take your money. Your goal from the first time we met was to be able to control your drinking. It has been five months and it's clear to you and all of us that it hasn't worked." I froze. Then I heard Shelley say, "Michael, I can't do this anymore."

Ray went on, "Shelley is here with Mark because the three of us are very worried. We want you to get better." (I understand now that this was what is called an intervention.)

I started to speak, trying to beg off with some lame excuse when Ray held up his hand to stop me.

"You love this woman, am I correct?"

I turned to Shelley. Both of us were crying. I said, "Yes" and meant it more than I had ever before.

Ray said, "Michael, it's really simple. You have one arm around the bottle and the other arm to steady yourself. There's nothing left for her."

No alcoholic wants to surrender what has kept him "safe" for years, but truth be told, I was tired of the deception, the lies, the hurt, and to be honest, I was tired of the drinking. I'd been doing it steadily for almost forty years! I had a decision to make. It was either Shelley or the bottle. I couldn't lose her. The problem was that I had made that promise so many times already. I was down to my last chance. I wanted to do it this time. I wanted to stop drinking and start our life together. Sure I wanted to do it for myself, but

I also wanted to do it for Shelley, for us. This was the only way she was going to stay with me. I just couldn't mess it up. I had to stop drinking NOW. I just wasn't sure if I could do it.

Ray handed me a piece of paper with the names of four treatment facilities. He said, "Choose one." Two days after Christmas, December 27, 1993, Shelley drove me to The Betty Ford Center in Rancho Mirage, California, a place we now refer to as Betty's house. I felt like a scared kid being dropped off at sleep-away camp. Neither of us knew what to expect. We didn't know if I would succeed, but we knew one thing for certain. We loved each other and we had hope. It was a silent, tense two-hour drive from Los Angeles to what would be my home for the next thirty days.

When we walked into Betty Ford, the man responsible for intake asked me when I had taken my last drink, which had been a week ago. He said I was one of the few people who hadn't shown up drunk. Apparently most see it as one last free-for-all. The hardest part was that I had to say good-bye to Shelley. I knew she would only be able to visit on the weekends and then only for three hours. No phone calls allowed. The focus is on recovery, and the program is very structured for a reason. But we were not used to being apart. I was more frightened about the separation than the actual work ahead of me. I didn't know what it would be like.

Chapter 15 - Betty Ford

After Shelley left, I was so lonely and afraid that I almost took off after her. Thankfully the guy that checked me in was a good guy and he understood. I'm sure he's seen a lot of shit in his time there. One of the first things that happens is you meet with a doctor. You are stripped naked and checked everywhere to be certain you aren't hiding any drugs, which I guess a lot of people try to do. You aren't allowed to even bring an aspirin with you or take anything unless a doctor gives it to you. They check your pulse, blood pressure, weight, and everything else to evaluate your overall health. I was glad I hadn't had a drink in about a week. I was lucky that for some reason I didn't suffer from the DTs or whatever it is you get when you suddenly are forced to dry out. I'd seen what that was like: the sweating, the hallucinations - even seizures. It can be horrible. I did have the anxiety, the insomnia, and the feeling of disorientation, or brain fog that comes with detoxing.

Everything at Betty Ford is very structured, something I had never had in my life. Hell, I thought I had been drafted. Generally you are assigned a room and a roommate. For some reason, I was lucky, because I had a private room. It was clean, orderly—a bed, a dresser, a chair—nothing fancy. That first night I didn't sleep at all. Then after what had seemed like two or three minutes, at about six thirty AM, someone was pounding on my door to wake me up for breakfast—a meal I hadn't been awake to see in twenty years! They had a nutritionist who made sure you were eating a balanced, healthy diet since many addicts pay little attention to that. And the daily routine started. After breakfast there were various meetings literally every hour until lunch. There was some free time, and then more meetings until dinner. It didn't take too long to get to know the guys in your group, and the camaraderie helped. Therapy sessions were serious, painful, and tough . . . but a bond was formed since we were all sharing our stories and the feelings that we were going through. It took three or four days for me to start to come out of the haze. That's when I began to face and deal with forty years of drinking and the toll it had taken: the anxiety, despair, hostility, inadequacy, defensiveness, sadness, loss, guilt, and grief I had buried in booze, not to mention the pain I had caused others. As it all came out, so did the tears for myself and for what these other guys had dealt with that brought us all to this place. It was tough, but it was good.

At the end of my first week, I developed a really sore big toe. I thought it was from the new sneakers I was wearing, but when it got so red, swollen and hurt like hell, I finally showed the doctor on staff. Initially they thought it was gout, a fairly common thing for an alcoholic. But when it didn't get better, I was taken to Eisenhower Medical Center. After a bunch of tests, they determined that I had developed osteomyelitis, which is a serious bacterial infection of the bone. I had to go on IV antibiotics twice a day, for the entire time I was in rehab (and for two months after I got out), which meant I had to get up an hour earlier than everyone else every morning - at 5:30 AM! I had no choice but to deal with it after they told me I actually could lose my foot. It sure didn't make things any easier, but the nurses were kind and understanding.

In spite of all this, there was some funny shit too. In the afternoons we had a meditation period—a time for relaxation and contemplation. I was so tired that one day I fell asleep and was snoring so damn loud I kept everyone else awake. Did I get teased about that! And how's this? One of my buddies kept stealing plates from the cafeteria and hiding them in his room. No reason—I guess he just liked plates. I think he had about seventy-five before they found out. Busted!

You were only allowed one phone call a week. That was torture. So this doctor from Toronto and I snuck down to the lobby one morning at about four AM and figured out a way to rig the phone. We hid behind the couch and called home every chance we could, whispering and giggling our asses off. Bad boys!

I grew to like and respect the guys in the group. One guy had been a helicopter pilot in Vietnam. He talked about his experiences there a lot. He and his buddy would land their chopper in an area in tall grass, flattening the weeds like a giant comb. Then the troops would scramble onboard to get the hell out of there under fire. He described the day he glanced over at his copilot to see his face was gone! He was able to rescue the other guys and make it out, but this haunting memory was eating him alive, and drinking was all he had to help him forget. After Betty's House, I heard he was doing well.

As I mentioned earlier, they put you on a special diet and make sure you are eating properly. I had to have a certain kind of muffin every day. I was standing in line to get breakfast and was digging around in the bread basket trying to find it when someone behind me said, "Have mine." I turned around and I'll be damned if it wasn't Mickey Mantle. Hell, I didn't want to eat it—I wanted him to sign it! After that, we would often sit together at the reflection pond by ourselves and just talk. It's amazing how this self-inflicted pain and evil you have in common flattens any divisions between you. Alcohol is the great equalizer. You and the others are all in the same boat.

Another time I was in line, once again for that elusive muffin, and someone behind me said, "Sorry, Michael. They will have more tomorrow." I turned around and it was Betty Ford. She was there often. She cared about this place that she built. After that, I even forgave her husband for pardoning Nixon.

The third week at Betty's House they had what's called "Family Week." Shelley and my daughter Jennifer came and stayed for this five-day program. We did not see each other at first. They were in a separate group led by trained therapists, with family members whose husbands, sons, fathers, or brothers were at Betty Ford trying to get clean. This intensive program was designed to help them learn about themselves, about co-dependency, and to unleash all their feelings of anger, pain, resentment toward the alcoholic. This all culminated on the fifth day when we came together.

The group sat in a big circle surrounding the family member, the person they were there for, who sat in the middle, face-to-face, knee-to-knee. Thankfully there were skilled therapists to guide us through this. It's impossible to describe what it feels like to be forced to hear how your behavior so profoundly affected the lives of those you love. It's brutally honest.

Jennifer recalled how when she was little, I was working day and night, and I was often on the road. When I was home, I was either drinking, drunk, or hung over. That's what Jenn remembered. There was constant tension between me and Paula. I would often rage or slam something or pass out, and Jennifer would beg for it to stop. She couldn't feel safe or secure in that environment, and as she told me example after example, she was sobbing. She admitted she was still afraid I would get angry right then and there. I felt so ashamed that this beautiful, innocent, sweet daughter of mine—the one I had wanted so desperately—was sitting here opposite me trembling. How much I had lost; how much she had been cheated of a father. Of course, there were many wonderful and loving memories, as when I would pick her up and put her little feet on top of mine and dance with her to a Johnny Ace song, but at this time, her pain poured out. To look in her eyes, hold her hands in mine, and tell her how sorry I was . . . I choke back tears even now when I think about it. All I could do was apologize again and again, and vow to make up for this by being sober.

It was hard enough to go through this once, but I had to do it twice, the next time with Shelley. Here is this woman I love; who had stuck by me despite all the heartache I had caused. I was forced to hear how much my selfishness had hurt her. To hear all the disappointment and embarrassment I had caused her. To hear her hopes and dreams for our life together were nearly shattered, and yet—she was here. If there was a moment that I truly knew I was ready to embrace sobriety, to humble myself, to take personal inventory and to make amends, it was then, looking into her beautiful brown eyes flooded with tears. I was so sorry. She believed me. She believed IN me. When we held each other in a long embrace, the entire room was crying.

It's raw, tough, grueling work. It takes courage. We were lucky we both held a belief in a power larger than ourselves. Some families who started out so hopeful don't make it through. Their relationships couldn't withstand it. I thank God every day that our relationship was strong enough to endure. I was so proud. I am so blessed.

Shelley stuck around that weekend so we could see each other on Sunday, visitors' day, before she drove back home. The final day of the Family Week was Friday, January 14th, her birthday. She was exhausted so she decided to treat herself to a spa day at a nearby hotel. I'll never forget when she came back Sunday afternoon all my buddies were so excited to see her and to wish her a Happy Birthday. They loved her too!

Shelley had taken off work to be at Betty's for those five days, which was not easy given her schedule. Since the cornerstone of Betty Ford is confidentiality, she refused to tell her boss anything other than it was a last-minute personal emergency. That didn't sit well with him, which caused her a lot of stress when she went back.

If that weren't enough, the day after she returned home, January 17, 1994, a 6.7 earthquake struck Los Angeles at about four AM She was alone, and it was terrifying, with multiple large aftershocks for days following. Our house got hit very hard, and she was left to try to make order out of chaos before my scheduled return the following week. When the quake hit, we actually felt it in Palm Springs, but I initially thought it was just a small one centered locally. Once the breaking news came about the mass destruction, I was desperate to hear her voice and to know she was ok. The lines were down, so it took a while, but we were finally able to get through to each other. She told me later it took all of her strength not to beg me to come home right then and leave Betty Ford. But more than anything, she knew our life together depended on my sobriety, and made up her mind nothing could get in the way of my completing the program. It took a lot of courage for her to do what she did—and a lot of love!

After the program ended, the real work began. Shelley and I had to basically hit the reset button. Would she like the new Michael? Would I be able to cope and enjoy life as a sober man? We both had to believe in the process and hope for the best. It was incredible to be back together, but I have to admit it took a while to adjust. We were cautiously optimistic, but we weren't quite as carefree at first.

We had to learn to trust each other all over again, but it made our relationship stronger. We relied on the Serenity Prayer, and took it "one day at a time." It took a little while before I was comfortable going out to dinner, or to places we used to go, but I wanted to. I wanted Shelley to have fun with me again, and to be out and about with her made me very proud. Much to my surprise, I didn't have a problem being around liquor. Shelley would always ask if it would bother me if she had a glass of wine or a cocktail, and if there was any hesitation, she didn't. Much to my surprise, I didn't want a drink. I liked the way I was feeling. I liked the way I looked. Slowly I was gaining back my self-respect.

One of the best things that happened to me when I got home was that I was asked to join a special AA meeting. It was a Monday night meeting, by invitation only, because it was composed of mostly "high profile people." This meeting had been founded by Dallas Taylor, a recovering addict who had been the drummer for Crosby, Stills, and Nash. There were a lot of musicians in the group and I enjoyed connecting with them as I was adjusting to this new life. There were also a number of famous actors. I used to laugh and say, "If you heard about some actor or musician in trouble on the news on Saturday, he'd be sitting at the meeting on Monday night!" It would be easy to be star struck walking into this meeting, but as my friend Denny told me, "Michael, in here, we are all just a bunch of drunks."

My heroes had always been famous drinkers . . . like Richard Burton. How he operated drunk I don't know. Burton could drink a bottle, give a flawless performance, never miss a line, and be so drunk afterward he couldn't stand up. I thought if I drank I could do the same. You think you can handle it, but it didn't fucking work. I was bullshitting myself.

There's a great story about Peter O'Toole and Richard Harris, two of my other idols. They were doing Shakespeare. The stage manager knocks on their dressing room doors for the five-minute warning before curtain. They aren't there! They are down the street at the local pub. He runs over there and finds them in full costume doing a scene. It was brilliant! "You're on now" he says, frantically pointing to Harris.

"Really? How am I doing?"

The stage manager grabs them both and they run down the alley, through the stage door. Richard is shoved on stage and trips right at the footlights, landing in front of a woman in the front row.

"Harris is drunk again," the lady sighs aloud!

Richard smiles at the woman and says, "Ah, just wait until you see O'Toole, Madam!"

I love these stories. It is the "romance" of these larger-than-life actors, giant talents that fueled my mistaken belief that drinking wouldn't get in the way of my art. That it could enhance it! Through this Monday night group, I learned that being an artist isn't an "excuse" for addiction. You don't get a free pass just because you are a "creative."

The support and camaraderie of the Monday night group kept me coming back. It took months for me to completely come out of the fog, but with their help, I did. There was a deep bond of understanding with these guys because we were united in the feelings of guilt. Our addiction had robbed us of the God-given talent that had fueled it in the first place. A vicious cycle. In the safety of that room we shared our fears, our failures, and a lot of laughter too.

In terms of my career, I knew it would be a struggle that would take time. I had to rebuild my image and prove myself. My reputation had caught up with me, and I was perceived as "risky." It also took a while to get my confidence back, to feel I was on solid ground and ready to put myself out there. A year went by without any success. Would I ever work again?

The first opportunity that came my way after I got sober wasn't exactly what I would have hoped for, but it was work, and it would be a huge test. In 1995 I was cast in a Telenovela that was shooting in Acapulco and Mexico City. It was a six-month commitment, and meant another separation from Shelley, but we agreed it was the right thing to do. When you are on location like that, the booze never stops flowing, and I wasn't sure how I would handle it. Most nights after shooting I would just go back to my room to avoid any temptation, and I was fine. It felt great to be in front of the camera sober! Three months in, Shelley came to Mexico City for a week.

It was wonderful having her there. I'll never forget, one night we were lying on the bed and we turned on the television. What are the odds of this? There was *The Mod Squad*, and Pete speaking in Spanish. (Shit, I can barely speak English.) It was hilarious!

After Shelley left, I missed her even more. I think my phone bill home was more than the national debt! I'm not sure I ever really proposed. We just decided that as soon as I got back we would get married. And we did, on February 25, 1996.

Our wedding was beautiful, intimate and perfect. It was at a gorgeous, historic hotel—the Huntington in Pasadena. We were surrounded by our family and closest friends—the people who had stood by us through the ups and downs and struggles we had gone through. It was made even more special because my nephew, Mike, a minister (and a talented actor in his own right), performed the ceremony. Jennifer gave a beautiful speech too, which made me very happy. We wrote our own vows, and when I looked in Shelley's eyes, nothing had ever felt so right. Of course, we both cried. There wasn't a dry eye in the room.

To come full circle, later that year, I was invited to return to visit my Australian friends, and this time Shelley would be with me. It had been quite a few years since the Logie incident, but I discovered that many of my old Aussie friends were still around. We shot a show called *Where Are They Now?* They had made arrangements to reunite me with the guy from the Royal Far West Hospital who I had "sponsored" during *The Mod Squad* years. Stephen was now a successful young man with a beautiful family of his own. We totally surprised him, sneaking through his neighbor's backyard and over the fence. His wife was in on it and had arranged to have him outside, grilling on "the barbie."

When I saw him, and called his name, he turned around, and we both damn near fainted! We also teared up, and hugged each other. I couldn't get over it. We met his entire family, ate lunch, and then in a private plane, we flew for a very emotional visit to the hospital in Manly where we had first met. It was beautiful sharing our memories as we walked along the beach, as if no time had passed.

I thought about my little Aboriginal friend, the child that I had danced with, and I learned she was doing just fine.

Chapter 16 - Sober

I had my sobriety and my incredible wife, but after our trip to Australia, my phone didn't exactly ring off the hook. I needed to find an agent to represent me, and that took a while. Again, I understood in some ways I was starting over again, and if that meant taking smaller roles, I was more than willing.

The first opportunity finally came when the wonderful Dick Van Dyke gave me a guest shot on his show, *Diagnosis Murder*. What a kind, gracious, and charming guy—a consummate professional, and so were all the people in the cast and crew. Next came a minor role on *Seventh Heaven*, which was another of Aaron's shows. Then there was a dry spell.

As frustrated as I was, I was sober, and had my three-year AA chip to prove it. *People* magazine approached me in 1999 about doing a story on me, my recovery, and putting my life back together. It wasn't easy for me to talk about, admitting after all those years that I had needed help, but it was time to go public. I wanted to share my journey in the hope that I could reach other people battling addiction. I wanted to give them hope. When the article came out, I received so much positive feedback that I knew I had done the right thing.

Not long after the article came out, I finally got a part that had some depth in a film called *The Apostate*. I played an evil monsignor in this crime drama set in San Juan, Puerto Rico. A priest goes undercover in the local art world in the hope of finding the serial killer who murdered his brother. It starred Dennis Hopper, and although I didn't have any scenes with him, it was truly an honor to watch him work.

In 2003 I had the great pleasure of reuniting with Clarence on his series, *Mystery Woman*. It was like old times. He was happy to see me sober, and I was proud, at long last, he could.

Just as I thought I was gaining some traction, lightning struck. You can never be prepared to learn you have cancer. When I heard the diagnosis, I literally went into shock and suffered what's called situational amnesia for a day. My brain couldn't process the words and just shut down. If ever I leaned on my buddy Christ, this was it. Thankfully with the help of skilled doctors, I had surgery and am cancer free. Shelley was there by my side throughout my recovery, helping to reassure me that I was not finished with life or my career! When she was diagnosed at the end of that same year, we were frightened all over again. Our prayers were answered when she too was cured. That's a chapter we were both glad to put behind us.

In 2006, I guest starred on an episode of *ER*, one of the finest series ever on television. I was cast as an alcoholic, in the hospital, suspected of hurting his wife in a drunken rage. You can only imagine how intense those scenes were, but I was back, and doing some serious acting.

In 2007, I had the great opportunity of working with Kevin Costner and Demi Moore in a motion picture called *Mr. Brooks*. It was a small role, but I particularly enjoyed meeting and hanging out a bit with Kevin. He is a gentle guy with a very big heart, and couldn't have been more supportive or encouraging about my working again.

Throughout these years, I would occasionally run into Aaron Spelling. The affection between us never truly changed, even though as I have said, I know I hurt him. Several years before his passing, there was a gala tribute in his honor. The cast members of his shows were all there: *Charlie's Angels, Beverly Hills 90210, The Love Boat, Seventh Heaven, and Dynasty*— the list goes on and on. The house was packed. I was asked to be one of the speakers, and it gave me the chance to thank Aaron from that stage, and tell him how much he meant to me. I said, "Aaron, I know I wasn't the best employee all the time, and I am sorry…but I love you." I spoke from my heart, and the audience responded with a rousing applause.

After the event, I went over to his table to say hello to Candy and to give Aaron a hug. We both cried. I am so grateful I had the chance to make amends to Aaron. That was the last time I saw him before he died.

You learn from the Twelve-Step program that making amends to those you have hurt is an integral part of sobriety. There were many people in my life that I wanted to apologize to. I call it "dying clean."

With Shelley's support, one of the first was Sharon. We were able to reconnect, and she was very happy to learn I was sober. I let her know how much I regretted the damage I had done to her and to our kids. Then I asked for her blessing to reach out to Candi and Jeff. I knew she had always been honest with them about the circumstances of my leaving, but I didn't know how she'd feel about my trying to contact them. She actually encouraged me to try.

There's a saying, "courage is fear that has said its prayers." After much introspection and many prayers, I found the courage to call. It was incredible to have that first conversation with Candi and later with Jeff. It was a little awkward in the beginning, but now I can say we have built a foundation of friendship and closeness. I think it has helped all of us to fill in a missing piece in our lives and be able to move forward.

The next step was reuniting in person. Jeff and I had been talking often for over a year when I had an occasion to go to Madison. I asked Jeff how he would feel about meeting, and he didn't hesitate. But as it got closer, and it became more real, we both admitted we were nervous! We finally decided to "just do it," like the Nike commercial. I will never forget that moment, Shelley and I standing in the lobby of the old Madison hotel, and seeing Jeff with his beautiful wife, Kelly, and their two sons, Riley and Sawyer . . . my grandkids! It was powerful. Since then we have gotten closer and closer.

The following evening Candi came over. It was hard to believe the last time I saw her she was a toddler in my arms, and now, some thirty years later, she was a grown woman. I told her stories about her as a baby, and she was warm and responsive.

Had it not been for sobriety, none of this would have happened. Sobriety is freedom. You are no longer a prisoner. You are free to work, to dream, and to love.

Love is what I feel when I think about Peggy and Clarence. After all these years, I can pick up the phone and call CW. He'll ask me, "Everything ok, Mick?" Or at our age, more often, it's "How's your health?" And the same goes for Peg. She holds a very special place in my heart. She still calls me Mick, too . . . for all the Irish in me. We catch up with each other often and there is such joy in sharing our lives and our memories so many years later. It is a testament to the connection the three of us had on our wild ride. I cherish them both, and of course Tige's memory.

I also treasure the amazing group of fans (my friends) that today still enthusiastically embrace *The Mod Squad*, and remain loyal to me. They are like a second family. They have created a *Mod Squad* and a Michael Cole page on Facebook, as well as a website and even a store with Michael Cole keepsakes. These folks remember every detail of the show. They can tell you how many times I twisted the ring I wore on the show, or the number of car chases, or when I wore a green shirt. I am so lucky they still care. It makes me feel that despite all the mistakes I made, I must have done a few things right!

In fact, recently my "friends" from Down Under, Studio 10, came all the way to Los Angeles to interview me. It was great fun reminiscing with them, and I'm told, the on-air piece got a terrific response from their viewers. Who knows, maybe it will get us back to Australia!

Epilogue

These days my mind wanders. And Shelley and I have done some wandering too. For her fiftieth birthday, we went to London and Paris. We were regular tourists, visiting Shakespeare's Old Globe Theater, Stonehenge, The London Museum, and The Whisper Gallery in the cathedral built by Christopher Wren. I loved all the history and the architecture. Paris was just as romantic as you might imagine. We took a boat down the Seine, went to the Picasso Museum, the Musée d'Orsay, the Rodin Sculpture Garden. We sat in a sidewalk café and watched the street painters near Sacre Coeur.

We celebrated Shelley's actual birthday with dinner at "Jules Verne," the restaurant atop the Eiffel Tower, the lights of Paris sparkling below. I arranged to have a bouquet of roses delivered to the table, and I'll never forget the look on her face. She carried it all the way back to the United States and we had it preserved and framed.

Over the years we have shared many adventures together, vacationing in Mexico, Hawaii, New York, Atlanta, the eastern seaboard, Maine, and Vancouver, Canada. Two years ago, we took a small ship through Alaskan waters and the inside passage. I never wanted to go on a cruise, but I have to admit this was spectacular—the scenery, the wildlife, and the ship itself. We met some terrific people from all over the country and had so much fun.

Shelley surprised me with a trip to Ireland. All my life, I have wanted to visit this beautiful and enchanting country. I romanced the atmosphere of the Irish pubs, listening to the likes of Dylan Thomas reciting the poetry. Shelley had every last detail arranged and presented me with the itinerary in a basket with the flag of Ireland, a can of Dinty Moore stew, and a map of the country. I was so touched, and so excited; but after all these years, something happened to me that had never happened before. That night, I had what's called a "drunk dream" where I saw myself drunk. It so frightened and unnerved me, and I knew I couldn't go. As disappointed as we were, we agreed that nothing is worth risking my sobriety. You can never take it for granted because "triggers" can sneak up on you if you aren't vigilant.

Sometimes, I find myself "traveling" in my mind, wondering about the Universe. I guess when I got sober I got sort of "cosmic." As I was reading Stephen Hawking's *A Brief History of Time*, with Carl Sagan's introduction, I noticed that Hawking, an avowed atheist, frequently mentioned God. That jumped off the page to me, since I had always been curious about how science and God could coexist.

Shortly after I met Shelley, I had a chance to ask that question to Carl Sagan. Shelley invited me to attend a business luncheon where Dr. Sagan was speaking. The majority of the people attending were from JPL—the Jet Propulsion Laboratory, and were there to hear him talk about the Voyager Spacecraft.

After Dr. Sagan spoke, he asked if there were questions. Many people asked about complicated, technical things which I didn't understand. I listened intently, all the while holding Shelley's hand under the table, palms sweating. Finally, I had to raise my hand, much to Shelley's surprise. I asked, "*In a Brief History of Time*, Hawking mentions God a lot. What do you think he meant by that?"

Dr. Sagan answered, "That's a good question. I believe that as long as there is something left for man to explore, to study and to learn, we will always refer to it as God."

Emboldened by my first question, I followed up . . . "Dr. Sagan, we have cracked and split the atom, and now we are down to the quark, which I think, in quantum physics is the smallest particle in the universe. And somehow, someday, we are going to split that and find what's inside. Then we are going to slap our foreheads and say—*Oh My God!* I have a feeling that's exactly what it's going to be!"

There was a beat, and Sagan nodded his head and said to me, "Thank you. I could never have put it more eloquently." That was my moment of enlightenment.

As we were making our way out of the ballroom, several people acknowledged me. I thought it was because they recognized me from *The Mod Squad*. Instead, they asked me where I was teaching - Cal Tech?!

That exchange with Carl Sagan was real, but I often have silent conversations with people in my mind. If only I could edit my memory. I find myself going back, as if maybe I could redo the dialogue, like they do when they "loop it" for TV, or retake a shot like they do on film.

There I am, sitting alone on the dock of the bay in San Francisco, watching leaves of different colors blowing in the wind. In my mind I saw them floating close to the shore at the Tenney Park lagoon in Madison. I wanted to get on one of those leaves and sail away. Where are they now? I remember almost everything, but it's as if I put all of those memories in the pocket of a special pair of old jeans I can't find anymore, but they're still around—somewhere. What if there are things in your pocket you can't remember putting there? Are they yours? Can you put voices and words in your pocket? Do they say the same thing though, when you take them out? When a rabbit runs through the snow and leaves its paw prints, are they there forever? Where does melting snow go? Maybe the stars (the celestial kind), are the only real thing. They were here long before all this "clock stuff."

Loneliness can still sometimes creep into my soul. I think some of it stems from a belief that the church abandoned me. Then, through all the alcoholic years, I abandoned it. I didn't need the church—I worshipped booze. Then Shelley's love came to be part of me, and with it, a renewed sense of the love of God—my buddy Christ.

You can buy a brick at Betty Ford with your name inscribed on it. We have one. That brick is the symbol of our new beginning, and of my sober life. We would not be together and I might not be alive if it weren't for Shelley and Betty! Maybe someone will see that brick and remember me and *The Mod Squad*. Maybe when they realize I went through addiction and came out the other side, it will give them the one thing an addict needs the most. Hope.

As for my career, the opportunities are fewer today. There aren't as many roles for a person my age, but I will never stop trying. I know I have more left to give. Besides, I have no choice; I am an actor; it's who I am. Things are done differently these days, thanks (or no thanks) to the internet. You get an audition and the sides one day and you are expected to get the scene on film and submitted the next. I miss having the luxury of time to immerse myself in a character and to meet with the casting people in person to discuss the part. I am learning to adapt, but it's not easy.

***

Every once in a while, I still think about the phone call I got from my biological father on the set of *The Mod Squad* all those years ago. It ignited a fire in me, the rage and pain that drove me down the path of self-destruction. Now I am able to look back and reflect on that, as well as all the other circumstances of my life, with the wisdom that time gives to all of us. What if I had met my father? Would that have changed anything? And the drinking? If I hadn't spent years lost in the bottle, would things have turned out the way they did? I battled the church, my stepfather, the system—anyone or anything that had authority over me. But without all those experiences, would I have found Shelley? Things have a way of working out the way they do for a reason. In God's time.

I'm reminded of an old saying - "there are no regrets in life, just lessons learned." If there's one thing I've learned from this crazy, tumultuous life, with its stratospheric highs and tragic lows, it's to live one day at a time. I have at last made peace with myself and let go of a lifetime of guilt and anger. I have the love of my wife, my beautiful Jennifer, and my family. I feel a tremendous sense of gratitude for the many blessings I have been given.

For the first time, things are truly the way they should be, according to God's plan, not mine.

Episodes and Fan Favorites

We had developed our own special formula on *The Mod Squad* and only a few other actors fit in. Aaron was very aware of that. It was important to have the right guest star, one who not only could handle the material, but who could also jell with the cast and keep the shooting on schedule. Not a lot of actors worked out, but luckily we managed to have so many great ones.

Richard Dreyfuss and I became friends and he was very professional. He played a suspected murderer and he was scary good. His character was attracted to Julie and wanted to get her involved in one of his schemes. He was very smart, but up to no good, and trying to get Julie to go along with him. But nobody touches Julie when Pete and Linc are around. I really respected Richard's talent. When I was having trouble with my drinking later on in my career, he was there. He said, "Michael, don't give up." I've always appreciated that support.

Ed Begley Sr. was there and he was an actor and a half. He was an Academy Award winner and he was doing *The Mod Squad*! I also got so excited when Jo Van Fleet, the woman who played James Dean's mother in the movie *East of Eden*, was on an episode in season three. To me she was a true heavyweight actor. I got goosebumps thinking about her being on the show. We got close and I couldn't believe I was acting with her. Ed Asner was on several times as well, including a two-parter in season five as an old cop. And we became great friends also.

Sugar Ray Robinson was another great guest that season. I couldn't believe it. My mother was a big boxing fan, and of course I am too. (Remember, I was in the Badger Boxer program as a kid! Me and boxing go way back.) Once I had taken Ma to Las Vegas and we went into a casino. "Look, Ma, at that guy in the pink tuxedo." It was

Sugar Ray Robinson. She said, "Is it really him?" I was so proud that I was able to walk up to him and he stood up to greet me. "Michael!" We hugged and I introduced my mother. She almost started to cry.

Leslie Nielsen was a lot of fun too. We hit it off right away. He was brilliant. He was Canadian and classically trained. Then he went into comedy. He was great in the show and we just bonded instantly. At the end of the episode, we are in Malibu under a bridge and the cops are looking for him. I try to get to him in time to warn him about the cops. I was under the bridge hiding from them when I heard the cars coming right at the ocean. "Oh shit." Then I hear gunshots and Leslie's character was hit!

He was the kind of actor who, even though he didn't have to work on location one day because it was just a phone scene where I was talking to him, he came in on his day off and read the scene with me. Of course there was no need for him to do that since he was off-camera, but he did it anyway. That was just amazing. That meant so much to me.

The other side of his personality was that he loved using those inflatable fart pillows. We'd be doing a big scene and I'd watch to see if his hands went near his pockets because you'd hear "Action," the scene would start, and he'd squeeze that fart pillow and break up the set. The crew was in hysterics. We went to Vegas once and several beautiful ladies circled us and started talking and flirting. Leslie introduced himself and acted very cordial toward them, and after he had charmed them, he would reach in his pocket and squeeze that damn pillow, making an audible sound. They would try not to act surprised, and he would just kept on talking and "farting."

"Oh, oops, sorry, ma'am. Please continue what you were saying." That was one of the many reasons I loved him.

I also loved Bo Hopkins; he was so funny. He'd always play a "hick" type of guy perfectly. In some of his lines, we just started laughing because of his ad-libs. Bobby Sherman was a good actor and much different than I would have thought. I wasn't too excited to have him on the show at first because, of course he was in teenybopper magazines and I didn't like that image. I was more interested in serious actors. I was probably more sensitive to him because the press often tried comparing the two of us. I was the cool rebel and he had a clean-cut image. At first, I wanted to distance myself, but later he proved to be quite an accomplished actor and we became friends.

My favorite episode of the entire five-year run of *The Mod Squad* was one called "Kristie." It was a Christmas episode. Pete's friend Jerry, a recent parolee, appears at Pete's door on December 23rd. He needs Pete to look after his young daughter, Kristie, for an hour while he tends to some business. After several hours, when Jerry hasn't returned, Pete grows concerned. He reveals to Linc and Julie that Jerry served time for being an accessory to a jewelry store robbery, and while he was in prison, his wife, Kristie's mother, was killed in a car accident. Since his release, Jerry had devoted himself to taking care of his daughter. He had given Kristie a big stuffed dog to keep while he was away, and she carried it with her everywhere.

What Pete didn't know was that inside that stuffed dog were the stolen jewels that the bad guys had hidden for safekeeping. Now the bad guys were hunting for the stolen jewels, and believed somehow Kristie had them.

On Christmas Eve day, with still no word from Jerry, Pete sets out with Kristie to look for her father. He stops at a church to buy a Christmas tree, and there, Kristie is drawn to a manger scene. She tells Pete that her mother had explained Christmas was about love, that God wanted to show us how he loved people.

That night, Julie and Linc came over to Pete's to watch Kristie while Pete continued to look for Jerry. When he comes back to his apartment, the three of them realize Kristie was missing and began a frantic search for her. Pete finds her at the one place he knew she would go—the Nativity Scene at the church. There is a tension-filled climax, and a happy ending.

Eventually Pete retrieves the jewels, catches the bad guys, and Kristie gets her stuffed dog back. Her dad is cleared of the charges and let go. They were reunited on Christmas morning. There are gifts under Pete's tree for Linc and Julie; Captain Greer is dressed as Santa Claus. In voice-over, viewers hear Pete recite the familiar first Christmas story from the Bible, Luke 2.

I don't think anyone would have expected a story of faith on a hippie cop show, but that's what we did. What also made this story my favorite was how tender the feelings were. I thought about my young daughter who I had left back in Wisconsin. In the scene on the first night when Kristie was left with Pete, I knelt down beside her to say our prayers, just as I had done so many years ago with Candi. I found myself welling up with tears, but I didn't want to cry in front of her. I tucked her into bed, kissed her goodnight, and it was exactly what I had done with my daughter. That's what "emotional recall" is—drawing from your own experiences. When it's real, the audience feels it too. That's why so many of my fan/friends say it's one of their favorites too.

There's something else I remember about this show. The young girl playing Kristie had several monologues that she had memorized. The director would stop shooting for one reason or another, and ask her to "pick it up" halfway through the scene to do another take. I didn't mind reshooting because she was adorable and trying very hard. "Ok, honey, just pick it up in the middle," the director said. Action! But she started at the very beginning. The director said, "Cut. I only want you to do *part* of the speech, not the whole thing. Action." She started at the beginning *again*, and I could see she was getting frustrated and anxious. All of a sudden I realized that this was the only way she had learned her lines. The only way she could deliver them. "Wait," I said, "she *has* to do it from the top. That's how she memorized it." I know it meant a lot that I was on her side. The next time the director said action, she did the entire monologue without missing a beat. We used that take because it was so touching. "Print that," I said.

If you are a parent or grandparent I hope you will think about this. Not all kids learn the same way. I had a problem as a boy in school which eventually led to my dropping out. It turns out I was dyslexic, which made learning very hard, as it had been for the young actress who played Kristie. If you sense a kid isn't happy in school, it might not necessarily be their fault. Check it out!

Another one of my favorite episodes was the one entitled "The Judas Trap" with Barry Brown. In this challenging role, Barry (one of the most promising young actors of the 1970s) was extraordinary as Dana, a mentally challenged boy cruelly victimized by his father.

Dana had autism—something that television had never addressed. Barry studied hard to perfect his speech so it would accurately depict his character.

In the story, Pete and Linc are running in the park when Pete notices a teenaged boy, still in pajamas, confusedly stumbling around. Pete approaches the boy, who recoils in terror. Pete determines that the boy, whose pajama top is bloody, is not mentally sound. The boy, seemingly in shock, is unresponsive. Pete invites the boy back with them to his apartment. There, Dana tells them that he excels at geography, has a good memory for faces, and counts cards when playing card games.

Pete offers Dana some clothes to wear home. When Dana removes his shirt, Pete and Linc are horrified to see welts on the boy's back. Dana admits his father beat him, but loyally still says his father is "really a great guy!"

Dana becomes the prime suspect when his father turns up murdered, but Pete didn't believe it. Dana needed someone he could trust; that someone was Pete. It is revealed for the first time in this episode that Pete had a brother with a mental disability who had passed away. This gave him even more compassion for this kid.

Pete took Dana to a rifle range for skeet shooting and was surprised to see that Dana was an excellent shot. Pete becomes horrified when Dana suddenly wails: "My father's dead! Somebody shot my father!" Hearing this, Pete began to have second thoughts about Dana's innocence, and when Dana finds out Pete is a "cop," he runs away. Eventually Pete finds the real killer, tracks Dana down, and gets him to the hospital.

The episode ends with Captain Greer handing Pete a letter from Dana, who is flourishing now in a special school. Pete reads out loud . . . "I never had a brother . . . but you are the one I would choose. I hope you feel the same about me . . . your friend, Dana." As I read those words, I held back tears. I am proud of this episode, and of Barry's performance. Sadly, a few years later I learned that Barry had killed himself. We lost a talented actor. I still miss him.

Watching "The Judas Trap" again after all these years, I flash back to my very first conversation with Aaron, when he told me that *The Mod Squad* was about *caring*. He was right.

Now that I've already offered some insights into some of my favorite shows, I'm including some memories and quotes from my "friends" about what the show meant and still means to them.

Fan Favorites:

"I Am My Brother's Keeper" (Season 4) This episode is almost exclusively Michael and he's quite simply brilliant. "Pete" has had a head injury and as he tries to solve a murder, he goes through a personality change that is so profound you almost don't recognize him as Pete . . . Michael takes "Pete" and turns him into someone else, again it is a brilliant performance.

– Jamie

"My, What a Pretty Bus" (Season 1) and "A Time for Remembering" (Season 2) stand out for me because the episodes were very moving, showing the depth of their feelings for each other. To this day I still recall the scene in "My, What a Pretty Bus" where Pete is initiating a group hug with Linc and Julie, declaring how much he missed them. In "A Time for Remembering" it was an intense episode, and with the declaration of the squad stating they are family radiated such love. *The Mod Squad* taught me empathy, compassion, and concern for others. I loved how the main characters respected and supported each other. I too wanted a friendship that Pete, Linc, and Julie had with each other. The show was thought-provoking too, as it covered controversial topics.

– Fran

"I like the show because it reminds me of my childhood. Many things bring back memories of a simple and happy time before the darkness of depression hit me. It was a time when we spent summers at the pool or riding bikes around the neighborhood. A time when we would play flashlight tag and catch fireflies. All the parents looked out for the kids. Peace signs and flowers were popular decorations. The colors of pea green and mustard yellow were popular

colors for walls. Yuck! I also like the relationship amongst the characters. In watching the shows from the 1st [to] the 2nd season, I can see the development of the characters and how they are more of a family unit. A scene that stood out recently was at the end of the episode. The character of Pete suddenly hugged Linc and Julie. Linc asked what's wrong or something along those lines. Pete said he was just happy to see them. I don't know if that was improvised or scripted, but it felt genuine and it was very touching."
 – Charlene

"The 60's. Black and white . . . dull, just the facts . . . one Tuesday night this thumping music and colors that I never heard or seen before . . . wow, just froze and stared for two hours. The actors . . . the script . . . everything was new and not my father's cop show. Even my parents watched with me. When I joined the fan group someone asked 'what's your favorite show?' Can't pick . . . like a child if you have more than one . . . every show is just killer."
 – Sharon

"My favorite episode is 'Yesterday's Ashes' (Season 5) because the girl was trying to find a new way of looking at life . . . to close one bad chapter and start a new one. Pete helped start her journey by telling her: *Yesterday was . . . just bury it. Today is.* When I watched this the first time I was at a very low place in my life. Pete helped the Sue character regain her self-respect by encouraging her to leave the past with all its nightmarish memories and decide who she wanted to be. She began to like herself. She changed. Pete helped her by surrounding her with supportive, healthy friendships with himself, Linc, and Julie."
 – Michelle

"I was only 6 when the show first aired, but watched it in reruns as a teenager. I had the biggest crush on Michael Cole, he had the sexiest smile I had ever seen. However, what I really loved about the show was the friendship these three shared. I have always wanted friends like this, ones that you know you can count on no matter what. The bond between these three made the show, perhaps because they were so close off-screen as well as on."

– Freda

"It was my favorite show as a child. Favorite episode is 'The Judas Trap' (Season 3), that's because of Barry Brown's wonderful performance."

– Greg

"I was a child of the 60's and just entering my teens when *The Mod Squad* came on. I loved the show because of the friendship and loyalty among the cast members. I can't really pick a favorite episode because I like them all. I have to say I still love Michael after all these years because he seems like such a dedicated, down-to-earth person who doesn't take friendships for granted."

– Dianne

"My very favorite show of all time! I loved every episode, but especially those that showed how they all grew together as a family such as 'A Time for Remembering,' 'The Exile' (Season 2), 'A Time of Hyacinths' (Season 3), and 'The Cave' (Season 4). Wonderful Show!"

– Wynne

"When *The Mod Squad* first aired on MeTV, and I saw the opening, I thought 'I remember this, this is familiar' and that's because my siblings watched. I was too young, but I remembered the opening . . . It would take forever to list all my favorites, but 'The Judas Trap,' of which I cry every time at the end; 'A Time for Remembering,' 'Kicks, Inc.' (Season 3), 'I Am My Brother's Keeper,' 'Sands of Anger' (Season 4), 'The Cave,' the one with the motorcycles, with Bobby Sherman guesting, the one with Leslie Nielsen guesting as Rusty. 'Cry Uncle' (Season 5) of which the ending gives me never-ending joy . . ."

– Ellyn

"I loved every episode. Truly. *The Mod Squad* was the perfect show for its time. My sister and I, along with our neighbor, used to play *The Mod Squad*. Of course I was always Pete (Michael). I can see us running in my backyard, arms interlocked, humming the theme song."
– Eileen

"*The Mod Squad* has and always will be my favorite show. My memories growing up with the show are precious to me. The show had a unique quality in the sense where it brought to our attention the many pressing issues with society. And the need to not turn your back on someone in trouble. It was clear how much the actors cared and believed in what the storyline was about. I couldn't imagine any other actors playing these roles. I think 'The Guru' (Season 1) was most special to me. The line Michael delivered was so powerful in response to the question 'Do you think I'm pretty?' 'You're beautiful. Do you have to be pretty too?' It shows how one can overcome emotional scars of hurtful things being said. It gave Daphne a new lease on life in believing in herself."
– Brian

"'Captain Greer, Call Surgery' (Season 1) and 'The Hot, Hot Car' (Season 3), 'Death of a Nobody' (Season 4) for starters. I love how the characters show love for one another. I also associate some of the places I've lived and jobs I've had with my viewing of the show. I just get a warm fuzzy feeling for *The Mod Squad*."
– Dan

"'The Cave' was a mini-movie, a complete psychological thriller. Awesome."
– Cindy

"I loved the very first episode, 'Teeth of the Barracuda!' Fell in love with 'Pete!' He was the ultimate rebel and resembled my husband!"
– Joyce

"My fav TV show of all time. It was hip, cool, different, and as a struggling teen in the late 1960s, I needed something hip, cool and different to escape to. Enter *The Mod Squad* to change my life forever! I identified with *The Mod Squad* (and Captain Greer too); each one in a different way. I had the biggest crush on Julie, with her 'class' and her beautiful, waist-length blonde hair. I loved each and every episode. I laughed, cried, and felt emotions and feelings I'd never felt before. On TV, I could feel the chemistry and love, and when I met all four in person, filming one summer day, on a Hollywood street, wow! For me, *The Mod Squad* has been, is, and always will be timeless, real, solid, and simply the best!"

– Joel

"*Mod Squad.* Those words used to stop time. For a shy, introverted young girl who struggled with the death of a parental figure they were the safety net that kept me from the abyss. Death and rejection could swirl around me but for one hour on Tuesday evenings at 7:30 my world shifted. Pete, Linc, Julie and the tough and tender Capt. Greer taught me that love could live in the broken places. And such a love. The fact that the three of them were outcasts resonated with me and the fact they loved each other without limits— hypnotized me. Unconditionally. The power of their relationship gave me hope that there was indeed something beyond pain. *Mod Squad* taught that you didn't have to be popular, perfect or tied by blood to be a family. They took each other as they were and never looked back. And, yes, they were fabulous to look at—the cool soul of Linc, the other world beauty of Julie, the crushing handsomeness of Pete and the ocean of security in Capt. Greer's eyes.

I would regain consciousness during a commercial break and realize that I was in my living room wearing my wildly striped *Mod Squad* bell bottoms. I wore them for every episode. I do not remember breathing as I watched. Lost. On the planet of *Mod Squad*.

Mod Squad addressed so many of the turbulent issues of the times and addressed them well but the true power of *Mod Squad* was in their bond—the family they became. This was and is their magic. It transcends the years. One white, one black, one blonde. One love."

– Linda

"I was a child of the 60's and just entering my teens when *Mod Squad* came on. I loved the show because of the friendship and loyalty among the cast members. I can't really pick a favorite episode because I liked them all. I have to say I still love Michael after all these years because he seems like such a dedicated down to earth person who doesn't take friendships for granted. Family, friends and animals seem to be a priority and I like that in a person. I got a good feeling about him when I was 12 and still have the same feeling at 60. Guess I just know a good thing when I see it."

– Dianne

"I am a member of the official Michael Cole page and wanted to share my love and respect for him. I was first introduced to the actor Michael Cole when the pilot of *Mod Squad* aired I was 15 yrs. old As most teenage girls I thought he was gorgeous and had his picture from a magazine on my wall. I have watched every episode and there is not one that I did not like. He has been my favorite actor since 1968.

"Some of my favorites are 'Eyes of the Beholder' with Janet Margolin. The way Michael looked at her and so gently cared for her was beautiful. 'A Run for the Money' with Lesley Ann Warren—at the end I will never forget when he walked out of the courthouse and talked with Lesley's character and they embraced as she walks away he looks at Julie and made a face that was smiling and embarrassed at the same time. It was just so sweet and innocent and I always felt he was such a method actor. 'Call Back Yesterday' with Anita Louise he showed so much love for his mother just the way he looked at her no words needed. 'I Am My Brother's Keeper'—Pete was hurt and had a bad head injury. He did it to perfection. You believed he was hurt. 'Deal With the Devil' with Leslie Nielsen—another emotional one with him trying to get through to his friend and at the end when he couldn't you could feel the pain he was going through. 'The Judas Trap' with Barry Brown is excellent acting by both actors and in 'Kristie' watching Pete with a child at Christmas was so sweet.

"For me whether it was *Mod Squad* or any of his other acting roles I never felt like it was Michael Cole acting. I just got into his role and he was who he was portraying. One of my favorite roles Michael played was a two-part *Love Boat*. He played Mike Kelly a paralyzed Vietnam veteran. He was amazing in this role he also did a *Fantasy Island* that had him as such a bad guy it was so different than so many roles he plays I just could not get over it. I don't know if you have ever seen a short called *Fathers' Day*. If not please watch it. Every time I have seen it I cry. The emotions, the look on his face the look in his eyes as he talks just breaks my heart. He is the real deal, a great actor. I wish I could find a copy of the *Dating Game* he was on no one seems to know how to get it.

"I believe it was 1968 or 1969 Michael guest hosted on a show, he was so down to earth and it was great to see the man Michael. I think you probably get the message that I am a huge fan. I must tell you that I grew up with law enforcement in my family so watching young hippies that were cops and did not carry guns and were not trying to bust people but to help them was so cool. (Groovy) as we used to say. On a personal note I had a very tough father and I remember way back watching Pete and saying at 15 that is the kind of guy that treats a girl right. I set my sights high as I wanted someone different than how I grew up. That was very powerful for a 15-year-old girl. I thank Michael for the way he portrayed Pete as it sure made a difference in my life. Oh I did marry that good guy I wanted and this Nov. we will be married 45 years."

– Carol

The following is a list of all of the shows we made and some of the guest stars that we had over the years. You'll notice the names become more recognizable as the series progresses.

Season 1

- The Teeth of the Barracuda (Sep. 24, 1968) – Fred Beir, Brooke Bundy (look for small roles with Harrison Ford and Richard Pryor)
- Bad Man on Campus (Oct. 1, 1968) – Norman Alden, J. Pat O'Malley
- My, What a Pretty Bus (Oct. 8, 1968) – Henry Jones, Byron Morrow
- When Smitty Comes Marching Home (Oct. 22, 1968) – Louis Gossett Jr., Valerie Allen
- You Can't Tell the Players Without a Programmer (Oct. 29, 1968) – Julie Adams, Mark Goddard
- A Time to Love – A Time to Cry (Nov. 12, 1968) – Robert Lansing, Harry Townes
- Find Tara Chapman! (Nov. 19, 1968) – Yvonne Craig, Della Reese
- The Price of Terror (Nov. 26, 1968) – James Best, Gail Kobe
- A Quiet Weekend in the Country (Dec. 3, 1968) – James Gregory, Ahna Capri
- Love (Dec. 10, 1968) – Nina Foch, Dee Pollock, Isabel Sanford
- Twinkle, Twinkle, Little Starlet (Dec. 17, 1968) – William Smithers, Robert Evans, Joan Van Ark
- The Guru (Dec. 31, 1968) – Dabney Coleman, Jane Elliot, Barry Williams
- The Sunday Drivers (Jan. 7, 1969) – Quentin Dean, Paul Carr
- Hello, Mother, My Name Is Julie (Jan. 14, 1969) – Nan Martin, William Windom
- Flight Five Doesn't Answer (Jan. 21, 1969) – Will Kuluva, Whit Bissell, Marvin Kaplan
- Shell Game (Jan. 29, 1969) – Michael Margotta, Jeff Pomerantz
- Fear Is the Bucking Horse (Feb. 4, 1969) – Ed Begley, Monte Markham

- A Hint of Darkness, A Hint of Light (Feb. 11, 1969) – Gloria Foster, John Milford
- The Uptight Town (Feb. 11, 1969) – Jason Evers, Cliff Osmond, Louis Gossett Jr., Barry Brown
- A Reign of Guns (Feb. 25, 1969) – J.D. Cannon, Sean Garrison
- A Run for the Money (Mar. 11, 1969) – Lesley Ann Warren, Tom Bosley
- Child of Sorrow, Child of Light (Mar. 18, 1969) – Ida Lupino, Daniel J. Travanti, Foster Brooks
- Keep the Faith, Baby (Mar. 25, 1969) – Sammy Davis Jr., Robert Duvall
- Captain Greer, Call Surgery (Apr. 1, 1969) – Edward Andrews, Kim Hamilton
- Peace Now—Arly Blau! (Apr. 8, 1969) – Christopher Connelly, Ross Elliott
- A Seat by the Window (Apr. 15, 1969) – Bo Hopkins, Julie Gregg

Season 2
- The Girl in Chair Nine (Sep. 23, 1969) – Cesare Danova, John Stephenson, Veronica Cartwright
- My Name Is Manolete (Sep. 30, 1969) – Rex Holman, Jean Byron
- An Eye for an Eye (Oct. 7, 1969) – Nancy Gates, Arthur Batanides
- Ride the Man Down (Oct. 14, 1969) – Richard Anderson, Brenda Scott
- To Linc – With Love (Oct. 21, 1969) – Janet MacLachlan, Fred Pinkard
- Lisa (Nov. 4, 1969) – Carolyn Jones, Arthur Franz
- Confrontation! (Nov. 11, 1969) – Simon Oakland, Robert F. Simon
- Willie Poor Boy (Nov. 18, 1969) – Joe Don Baker, Daniel J. Travanti
- The Death of Wild Bill Hannachek (Nov 25, 1969) – Murray MacLeod, Tim O'Kelly, Tyne Daly

- A Place to Run, A Heart to Hide In (Dec. 2, 1969) – Don DeFore, Tom Tully
- The Healer (Dec. 9, 1969) – Paul Richards, Dwayne Hickman
- In This Corner – Sol Alpert (Dec. 16, 1969) – Marvin Kaplan, Noam Pitlik
- Never Give the Fuzz an Even Break (Dec. 23, 1969) – Maurice Evans, Harriet E. MacGibbon
- The Debt (Dec. 30, 1969) – Peter Brown, Nehemiah Persoff
- Sweet Child of Terror (Jan. 6, 1970) – Martine Bartlett, Dennis Patrick
- The King of Empty Cups (Jan. 20, 1970) – Noel Harrison, Simon Scott
- A Town Called Sincere (Jan 27, 1970) – Tom Stern, Ford Rainey
- The Exile (Feb 3, 1970) – Nico Minardos, Lawrence Dane, James Sikking
- Survival House (Feb. 10, 1970) – Sammy Davis Jr., William Smithers
- Mother of Sorrow (Feb. 17, 1970) – Lee Grant, Richard Dreyfuss
- The Deadly Sin (Feb. 24, 1970) – Lynn Loring, Bert Freed
- A Time for Remembering (Mar. 3, 1970) – Gary Vinson, Richard Eastham
- Return to Darkness, Return to Light (Mar. 17, 1970) – Gloria Foster, Ivan Dixon
- Call Back Yesterday (Mar. 24, 1970) – Margot Kidder, Anita Louise, Mark Goddard
- Should Auld Acquaintance Be Forgot (Mar. 31, 1970) – Frank Converse, Ed Asner
- The Loser (Apr. 7, 1970) – Diana Muldaur, Frank Aletter, David Cassidy, Marion Ross

Season 3
- The Long Road Home (Sep. 22, 1970) – Anjanette Comer, Lou Antonio
- See the Eagles Dying (Sep. 29, 1970) – Lane Bradbury, Paul Carr

- Who Are the Keepers, Who Are the Inmates? (Oct. 6, 1970) – Richard Kiley, Booth Colman, Meg Foster
- "A" Is for Annie (Oct. 13, 1970) – Jo Van Fleet, Ron Hayes
- The Song of Willie (Oct. 20, 1970) – Sammy Davis Jr., Lola Falana
- Search and Destroy (Oct. 27, 1970) – Steve Ihnat, Michael Baseleon
- Just Ring the Bell Once (Nov. 3, 1970) – Brian Dewey, Mittie Lawrence
- Welcome to the Human Race, Levi Frazee! (Nov. 10, 1970) – Cal Bellini, Edgar Buchanan, Bo Svenson
- A Far Away Place So Near (Nov. 17, 1970) – Ben Murphy, Michael Margotta, Bo Hopkins, James Sikking
- A Time for Hyacinths (Dec. 1, 1970) – Vincent Price, Charles McGraw
- The Judas Trap (Dec. 8, 1970) – Don Porter, Barry Brown
- Fever (Dec. 15, 1970) – Robert Viharo, Frank Maxwell
- Is There Anyone Left in Santa Paula? (Dec. 29, 1970) – Fernando Lamas, Victor Millan
- A Short Course in War (Jan. 5, 1971) – Ben Balaban, Josephine Hutchinson
- Kicks Incorporated (Jan. 12, 1971) – Jack Cassidy, Barbara Rush, Danny Thomas
- A Bummer for R.J. (Jan. 19, 1971) – Carl Betz, Daniel J. Travanti, Annette O'Toole
- The Hot, Hot Car (Jan. 26, 1971) – Greg Mullavey, Robert Donner
- Suffer, Little Children (Feb. 9, 1971) – Kaz Garas, Sheldon Allman
- Is That Justice? No, It's the Law (Feb. 16, 1971) – Nehemiah Persoff, Burr DeBenning
- A Double for Dinner (Feb. 23, 1971) – Michael Ansara, Ray Walston
- Welcome to Our City (Mar. 2, 1971) – Billy Bowles, Virginia Gregg
- The Comeback (Mar. 9, 1971) – Sugar Ray Robinson, Hilly Hicks, Rocky Graziano, Dick Enberg
- We Spy (Mar. 16, 1971) – Rene Auberjonois, William Smith

- The Price of Love (Mar. 23, 1971) – Paul Richards, Clint Howard

Season 4
- The Sentinels (Sep. 14, 1971) – Scott Marlowe, Hal England
- Cricket (Sep. 21, 1971) – Lee Montgomery, Susan Howard
- Home Is the Street (Sep. 28, 1971) – Cameron Mitchell, Brooke Bundy
- Survival (Oct. 5, 1971) – John Rubinstein, Karen Ericson
- Color of Laughter, Color of Tears (Oct. 12, 1971) – Ed Asner, Anne Archer
- The Medicine Man (Oct. 19, 1971) – Robert Foxworth, Lou Antonio, Billy Dee Williams
- The Sands of Anger (Oct. 26, 1971) – Shelly Novack, Arthur Franz, Tony Dow
- The Poisoned Mind (Nov. 2, 1971) – Laraine Stephens, Jack Collins
- Exit the Closer (Nov. 9, 1971) – Larry Blyden, Ruta Lee
- Whatever Happened to Linc Hayes? (Nov. 16, 1971) – Lance Taylor Sr., Lee deBroux
- And a Little Child Shall Bleed Them (Nov. 23, 1971) – Milton Berle, Keenan Wynn
- Real Loser (Nov. 30, 1971) – Martin Sheen, Harold Gould
- Death Of a Nobody (Dec. 7, 1971) – Perry Lopez, Meg Foster
- Feet of Clay (Dec. 14, 1971) – Desi Arnaz Jr., Robert Donner, Kevin Dobson
- I Am My Brother's Keeper (Jan. 4, 1972) – Linda Marsh, Guy Stockwell
- Deal With the Devil (Jan. 11, 1972) – Leslie Nielsen, Bill Fletcher
- Kill Gently, Sweet Jessie (Jan. 18, 1972) – Al Freeman Jr., Glynn Turman, Leslie Uggams
- Shockwave (Jan. 25, 1972) – Michael Anderson Jr., Lynn Loring
- No More Oak Leaves for Ernie Holland (Feb. 1, 1972) – Robert Pine, Cal Bellini
- The Cave (Feb. 8, 1972) – Karl Swenson
- Wild Weekend (Feb. 15, 1972) – Brenda Scott, Stephen Young

- The Tangled Web (Feb. 22, 1972) – John Calvin, Woodrow Parfrey
- Outside Position (Feb. 29, 1972) – Bobby Sherman, Judy Strangis
- Big George (Mar. 7, 1972) – Andy Griffith, Sharon Acker

Season 5
- The Connection – Part 1 (Sep. 14, 1972) – Ed Asner, Bradford Dillman, Cleavon Little, Stefanie Powers, Richard Pryor, Robert Reed, Cesar Romero
- Connection – Part 2 (Sep. 14, 1972) – Cleavon Little, Richard Pryor
- The Thundermakers (Sep. 21, 1972) – Bobby Sherman, John Lasell
- Yesterday's Ashes (Sep. 28, 1972) – Jo Ann Harris, Robert Pine
- A Gift for Jenny (Oct. 5, 1972) – Paul Richards, Bo Svenson
- Taps, Play It Louder (Oct. 12, 1972) – Peter Hooten, Michele Nichols
- Eyes of the Beholder (Oct. 19, 1972) – Janet Margolin, Beverly Garland
- Good Times Are Just Memories (Oct. 26, 1972) – Leif Erickson, Tyne Daly, Sam Elliott
- Corbey (Nov. 2, 1972) – Nehemiah Persoff, Simon Scott
- Can You Hear Me Out There? (Nov. 9, 1972) – Louis Gossett Jr., Carl Bellini
- Another Final Game (Nov. 16, 1972) – Clu Gulager, Beverlee McKinsey
- Crime Club (Nov. 23, 1972) – Robert Lipton, Pamela Susan Shoop
- The Twain (Nov. 30, 1972) – Fritz Weaver, Victoria Racimo, Vic Tayback
- Belinda – The End of Little Miss Bubble Gum (Dec. 7, 1972) – Catherine Burns, Bob Balaban
- Kristie (Dec. 14, 1972) – Michael Anderson Jr., Debbie Lytton
- Sanctuary (Dec. 21, 1972) – Glenn Corbett, Hal England, Victor Buono

- Run, Lincoln, Run (Jan. 4, 1973) – James A. Watson Jr., Elliott Street
- Don't Kill My Child (Jan. 18, 1973 – Marilyn Mason, Murray MacLeod
- Death In High Places (Jan. 25, 1973) – Fernando Lamas, Jim Backus, Ahna Capri
- Put Out the Welcome Mat for Death (Feb. 1, 1973) – Martha Scott, Howard Duff, James Sikking
- Scion of Death (Feb. 8, 1973) – Don Porter, Julie Adams
- The Night Holds Terror (Feb. 15, 1973) – Richard Dreyfuss, Brooke Bundy
- Cry Uncle (Feb. 22, 1973) – Theodore Bikel, Gino Conforti, Geoffrey Lewis, Kathleen Freeman
- And Once For My Baby (Mar. 1, 1973) – Ed Nelson, Linda Marsh

Acknowledgements

I want to thank the many people over the years who said, "You should write a book"! All those seemingly small comments truly helped. They made me believe I had a story to tell, and gave me the kick in the ass to get started.

Thank you to my family who encouraged me every step of the way. Their love and support mean everything. A shout out to Mike Caldwell, who spent a lot of time proofing my poor spelling and punctuation, and to Allen and Joy Goldblatt, who devoted hours recording and transcribing.

And to these special people: (I hope I won't forget anyone!!!)
-Peggy Lipton, my soul friend.
-C.W.III, always there.
-Adrian Carr, film director and the photographer who brought the Cover to life with his photo.
-Barbara Anderson, talented editor, and incredible advisor.
-Dr. Elaine Bridge, who taught me so much about myself.
-Doug Moe, formerly of the Wisconsin State Journal, who read my first "pitch".
-Bill Zehme, author of the New York Times bestselling homage to Frank Sinatra, The Way You Wear Your Hat, who told me what I had written was "raw and authentic", and to keep that voice.
-Breanna K, who worked tirelessly to help get the pictures in to the book.
-Casey Green, for technical and moral support.
-Stephanie and Bryan Whitehead, and the Official Michael Cole Fan Group.
-Greg and Lesley Fermin, and The Mod Squad Group Fan Page.
-Wayne Shulman, Calvin Spiker who attempt to "handle" me.

Last but not least, without the persistence of Diane Nine, my literary agent, and the patience and talented writing skills of Dave Smitherman, there wouldn't be a book. My heartfelt gratitude to them, and to Bear Manor Media for Publishing "I Played the White Guy".